PURSUING
HOLINESS
IN THE LORD

Jonathan Edwards for Today's Reader

T. M. MOORE, SERIES EDITOR

Also in this series:
Growing in God's Spirit
Praying Together for True Revival

PURSUING

HOLINESS
IN THE LORD

JONATHAN
EDWARDS

EDITED *by* T. M. MOORE

INTRODUCTION *by*
ROBERT M. NORRIS

P&R PUBLISHING
P.O. BOX 817 • PHILLIPSBURG • NEW JERSEY 08865-0817

Page design by Tobias Design
Typesetting by Lakeside Design Plus

Printed in the United States of America

Library of Congress Cataloging-in-Publication Data
Edwards, Jonathan, 1703–1758.
    Pursuing holiness in the Lord / Jonathan Edwards ; edited by T. M. Moore ; introduction by Robert M. Norris.
      p. cm. — (Jonathan Edwards for today's reader)
    Includes bibliographical references and index.
    ISBN-10: 1-59638-012-8 (pbk.)
    ISBN-13: 978-1-59638-012-7 (pbk.)
    1. Holiness—Christianity—Early works to 1800. 2. Christian life—Congregational authors. I. Moore, T. M. (Terry Michael), 1949– II. Title.

BT767.E39 2005
234'.8—dc22

                                  2005049439

To

James A. R. Johnson

CONTENTS

Series Introduction   ix

Editor's Preface   xv

Introduction by Robert M. Norris   I

Part 1: The Character of Paul an Example to the Christians

1 A Call to Imitate   13

2 Seeking the Good of Our Souls (1)   21

3 Seeking the Good of Our Souls (2)   31

4 The Virtues of Paul toward God   39

5 The Virtues of Paul toward Men   53

6 The Virtues of Paul toward God and Men   61

7 Following Paul's Example   81

Part 2: Hope and Comfort Usually Follow Genuine Humiliation and Repentance

8 Hope and Comfort at Conversion   99

9 Hope and Comfort for the Christian   119

10 Reasons for This Doctrine   141

11 Application of the Doctrine   151

Part 3: The Preciousness of Time and the Importance of Redeeming It

12 The Preciousness of Time   173

13 Improving Time   187

    Index of Scripture   197

SERIES INTRODUCTION

Jonathan Edwards (1703–1758) is one of the great figures of American church history. Pastor, theologian, evangelist, missionary, husband, and father, Edwards was mightily used of God in his day, and his written works continue to instruct and nurture those who take the time to study them in our own. During his tenure as pastor in the Congregational church in Northampton, Massachusetts, Edwards's preaching was the catalyst God's Spirit used to ignite two powerful seasons of revival, including the Great Awakening of the 1740s. He was a man of the Book and a man of the church, devoting himself to the study of God's Word and the work of pastoral care and edification in congregations in New York City, Northampton, and Stockbridge, Massachusetts, where he served as a missionary to Native Americans. Although he was elected president of Princeton College in 1757, his untimely death made his tenure there all too brief.

This series is devoted to bringing the sermons and other works of Jonathan Edwards to today's readers in a form that can make for careful reading, thoughtful consideration, lively discussion, and significant growth in the grace and knowledge of the Lord. Edwards preached to farmers and merchants, homemakers and youth, Native

Americans and small-town professionals. Although his language can seem at times obscure and the logic of his arguments demands our diligent attention, the ordinary people of his day understood him quite well. For nearly three hundred years the works of Jonathan Edwards have instructed and inspired pastors, theologians, and lay readers to a greater love of God and more diligence in spreading God's love to others. This suggests that Edwards's works can serve us in our generation as well.

Edwards's sermons and books are steeped in Scripture and employ careful exposition and rigorous logic to make the glory of the gospel of Jesus Christ clear and compelling. His was indeed a "rational Biblical theology," to borrow a phrase from Dr. John Gerstner, to whom contemporary Christians owe a great debt for his tireless promotion and exposition of the works of the greatest theologian ever to grace the American ecclesiastical scene. For a variety of reasons—among them the demanding nature of Edwards's writing; his use, at times, of archaic or unfamiliar terms; and the difficulty of procuring his works—contemporary readers have not availed themselves of Edwards's sermons and books as much as they might. To their enormous credit, the editors and publishers of the Banner of Truth Trust have labored to overcome these difficulties by making a large number of Edwards's works available in two hefty volumes and by publishing individual sermons and books as separate publications. We are grateful to the Trust for granting us permission to use the edition of Edwards's works prepared by Edward Hickman, first published in 1834 and kept in print by Banner since 1974, for the texts in this series.

The books in this series present the works of Edwards in their original form, as prepared by Hickman, without significant modification in his language. At times we have updated the spelling of a word, altered punctuation, or included Scripture references that Edwards omitted in his texts. We have added headings and subheadings to clarify his arguments, divided some long paragraphs, and portioned each work into short chapters to allow for more careful and considered reading. We have also incorporated study questions at the end of each chapter to promote thoughtful reflection on the meaning and application of Edwards's arguments and to encourage use of his works in reading and discussion groups.

This series is prepared under the sponsorship of the Jonathan Edwards Institute, whose mission—to promote and nurture a God-entranced worldview—mirrors that of Edwards. We are grateful to Allan Fisher and the staff of P&R Publishing for their vision for and commitment to the plan and purposes of this series. Our hope is that the books in this series will introduce Jonathan Edwards to a new generation of readers and draw them more deeply and passionately into the knowledge of God. We offer them with the hope that God, who sent the Spirit of revival to his church in Edwards's day, might be pleased to use this series as he moves to revive, renew, and restore his glory in his Bride once again.

T. M. Moore
The Jonathan Edwards Institute

A series of volumes dedicated to the memory of one of whom many people are unaware needs some explanation. Yet those who have known Jim Johnson understand at once why an exploration of the thought of Jonathan Edwards is a fitting tribute.

Jim was a husband to Martha and father to three sons, Mark, Steve, and David, who are dedicated followers of Christ. He was the mentor and encourager of untold numbers of young men in every walk of life and served as an elder in his church, the Fourth Presbyterian Church in Bethesda, Maryland.

Jim possessed many intellectual qualifications. He was trained in the liberal arts, and he possessed a doctoral degree in jurisprudence. Far from living in academic isolation, he also held various positions within American corporate life, and he worked and moved with ease in government.

He was fully aware of the reality of the fallenness of our humanity. He lived with it and experienced some of its harshest dealings. Yet to each of his callings, and in all his experiences, Jim brought a devotion to Christ and a love of truth. He was an example of one who sought to bring all of life captive to the Word of God.

Jim Johnson serves as a model to those who seek to harness a vital, living relationship with Christ with an honest pursuit of working that out with theological integrity and ethical rigor. When faced with the diagnosis of inoperable cancer, he showed that, as Jonathan Edwards often remarked, Christians can die well. Like Edwards's faith, Jim's was real, true, and practical, and it demanded to be worked out in intellectual, experiential, and ethical ways.

Redeemed by Christ, Jim lived life in gratitude, which is why each one of us who knew him mourned the passing of a great encourager, a powerful mentor, and a humble servant of the Lamb.

Robert M. Norris
Senior Pastor
Fourth Presbyterian Church
Bethesda, Maryland

Editor's Preface

With this, the third volume in our series Jonathan Edwards for Today's Reader, it seems a good time to reflect on the progress of this series to date. The first two volumes focused primarily on the work of God's Holy Spirit in bringing faith, growth, and revival to his people. *Growing in God's Spirit* examined Edwards's view of the role of the Holy Spirit in bringing new life to lost sinners and in helping them to make progress in the life of faith. Of course, that volume also looked at the believer's responsibility in the matter of Christian growth; however, the primary focus was on the work of God's Spirit in shining a divine and supernatural light into the hearts of his people, and opening up the vision of life as a pilgrimage to glory, so that the followers of Christ might know him and grow in the grace and knowledge of the Lord.

In the second volume, *Praying Together for True Revival* (Edwards's book, *An Humble Attempt*), we saw how the Spirit works to call God's people together to pray that he will send his Spirit with renewed power and glory to revive his people and awaken the lost to the salvation that is in Jesus Christ. Again, the people of God have a duty before the Lord to come together in united, explicit, extraordinary prayer for the revival of true religion. But even this is the work of God's Spirit, as must be the sought-for revival.

In this third volume we begin to explore more pointedly Edwards's teaching concerning the believer's responsibility for growing in the life of faith, beginning with his or her role in God's work of sanctification. Once again God and his grace take center stage—as in all of Edwards's works—as the great Northampton preacher leads us through three sermons showing how God is pleased to work out his salvation in the lives of those who love him. But the primary focus is on what God requires of us—how we must take up our duties and make the most of every opportunity for improving our relationship with Jesus Christ.

In a day when, over and over, we hear that Christians are not all that different from their unbelieving contemporaries at expressing their faith in everyday life, it is important that we understand and take up our calling to pursue holiness in the Lord. The Scriptures make this call in many ways: we are to work out our salvation in fear and trembling, to pursue holiness in the fear of the Lord, to be holy as God our Father is holy, to grow in the grace and knowledge of the Lord Jesus Christ, to run the race that is set before us with our eyes fixed on Jesus, to press on, to do good as often as we have opportunity, to bear fruit that will abide, and so forth. There is no getting around the biblical teaching that being a Christian means that we are to be *different* from those around us who are not. Christians are to be the light of truth in a world of relativism and darkness, a leaven of goodness in the loaf of a sinful world, the salt of the earth, and a city set on a hill for all to see. That we are all too often *none* of these things leaves us vulnerable to charges of hypocrisy and irrelevance, and makes our proclamation of the Good News of Jesus a matter of indifference, or even scorn, to a world searching for something substantial in which to hope.

Edwards's call to pursue holiness in the Lord, therefore, could hardly be more timely. As we begin to look more pointedly at Edwards's teaching concerning the life of faith, we trust that this third volume in the series Jonathan Edwards for Today's Reader will mark out a path that many will take up anew with fresh vision and commitment. The call to holiness is an invitation to the path of blessedness, comfort, and joy in the Lord. It is not an easy path, and we may often stray from it into the wilderness of sin. However, the duty remains for each believer to consider how we may begin to make better use of our time, redeeming more and more of it for the work of the kingdom and the pursuit of holiness in the Lord. Without such a commitment, the life of faith is shallow and unfulfilling at best, nonexistent at worst.

Let Edwards's call to pursue holiness in the Lord catch you up in a new way in the walk of faith. And, for those of you just joining us in this series, may it lead you to seek Edwards's guidance and encouragement in the other volumes of our series as well.

T. M. Moore

INTRODUCTION

All of us, at some time or another, have to ask ourselves the great questions of life, such as, Who am I? and Why am I here? These are questions to which every Christian has found answers. We know that, by faith, our true identity is to be found "in Christ." Through his sacrifice on the cross of Calvary, we have been reconciled to God, and we are now adopted into the family of God. Our purpose now is to live always to the praise and glory of God.

Understanding and living the Christian life—what Scripture refers to under the idea of "sanctification"—lay at the core of the preaching of Jonathan Edwards. Because this is the case, his work continues to make an impact upon believers in every generation. His practical outworking of issues is soundly based upon a firm theological understanding. In our generation there are few things more necessary than to grasp again the great doctrine of sanctification. In the three sermons that are contained in this volume, we see the theologian and the pastor marrying truth and application in a way that gives his work its timeless quality.

Edwards knew from his own experience that loving Jesus lies at the heart of the way in which our practical obedience to him is worked out. It is what makes the Christian life a life of love and not simply one of duty. Edwards wrote eloquently of this in his "Personal Narrative":

> Holiness, as I then wrote down some of my contemplations on it, appeared to me to be of a sweet, pleasant, charming, serene, calm nature. It seemed to me it brought an inexpressible purity, brightness, peacefulness and ravishment to the soul: and that it made the soul like a field or garden of God, with all manner of pleasant flowers; that is all pleasant, delightful and undisturbed; enjoying a sweet calm, and the gently vivifying beams of the sun. The soul of a true Christian, as I then wrote [in] my meditations, appeared like such a little white flower as we see in the spring of the year; low and humble on the ground, opening its bosom to receive the pleasant beams of the sun's glory; rejoicing as it were in a calm rapture; diffusing around a sweet fragrancy; standing peacefully and lovingly in the midst of other flowers round about; all in like manner opening their bosoms to drink in the light of the sun.
>
> There was no part of creature-holiness that I then, and at other times, had so great a sense of loveliness of, as humility, brokenness of heart and poverty of spirit: and there was nothing that I had such a spirit to long for. My heart as it were panted after this, to lie low before God, and in the dust: that I might be nothing, and that God might be all; that I might become as a little child.[1]

1. Samuel Hopkins, *The Life and Character of the Late Reverend Mr. Jonathan Edwards* (Boston, 1765), 29–30.

In each of the works that are included in this, the third volume in the series Jonathan Edwards for Today's Reader, we see some of the important truths of the doctrine of sanctification made clear. Edwards reminds us with pointed clarity that practical sanctification is intimately and indispensably dependent upon the union of the believer to Christ. With the apostle Paul he makes clear that all of our spiritual life, both its origination and its continuance, springs from our spiritual union with Jesus Christ. He recorded in his diary on Saturday, December 22, 1722: "This day, revived by God's Holy Spirit; affected with the sense of the excellency of holiness; felt more exercise of love to Christ than usual. Have, also, felt sensible repentance for sin, because it was committed against so merciful and good a God."

Gratitude for life in Christ draws out of the believer a desire for holiness, even as it creates in the believer a healthy hatred of the sin that mars our life and disfigures us.

It is because Jesus Christ has lived the life that we should have lived—a life of obedience to the law of God—and because he has died the death that we deserved—because of our failure to keep the commands of God—that we are accepted by God. The constant theme of the whole of the Scripture is the gospel. Scripture also makes clear that our faith is not a work. Our new status is based wholly on the merits of Christ and not on anything about us. While a paintbrush may be the *instrumental* cause of a work of art, the *real* and *efficient* cause is, of course, the painter. In the same way, while faith may be the *instrumental* cause of our union with

Christ—that which brings about salvation—the *real* or *efficient* cause—that which is finally responsible for salvation—is God.

In Edwards's sermon "The Character of Paul an Example to the Christians," we are shown the importance of seeking the salvation of our souls in Jesus Christ alone. The urgency and intensity with which we pursue this goal never obscures the fact that it is in Christ and not in our efforts or merit that salvation is secured. In fact, Edwards urges us to follow Paul in looking away from our works. The apostle makes clear that being a Christian demands a change of attitude not only to our sin, but also to our righteousness. The gospel and it alone is the source of our life and our assurance. With the great apostle we must be adamant that any change to the gospel, no matter how small that change may be, will result in massive distortions in our understanding and spiritual experience. In fact, any change will result in the gospel being no gospel at all. Edwards points us to the very core of what we believe.

However, Edwards also makes clear that the gospel is no dead thing; rather it is alive, and he reminds us that we must always be applying the gospel to our lives. With this emphasis he assists us in recognizing and avoiding the twin dangers of rationalism and mysticism. Too easily some Christians move from a living relationship with Christ to an emphasis upon preserving the truth. Undoubtedly the gospel is profound doctrine, but it is truth about grace; it is alive and cannot be confined to the realm of the intellect alone. The gospel is not merely an exercise in *rational* thought.

What is also true is that some Christians move to the other extreme, where a relationship with Jesus Christ is understood in solely mystical terms, and faith is divorced from content or action and confined to the realm of *experience* alone. Edwards shows us in this sermon that the gospel is alive. We do not simply learn it when we are converted and then move on from there. The example that Paul offered to the Philippians was of a strength in faith that grew out of a love for Christ. It manifested itself in prayer, praise, and a contentment with the mysterious actions of providence in life. Edwards shows us that the gospel is the *continual* need of the believer. Sanctification is about the gospel working itself out in the life, experience, and witness of the Christian. He shows us the fallacy of restricting the gospel to conversion alone. Yet today there are many who in practice see the gospel as necessary to find Christ and then see growth in the Christian life as a matter of hard work and obedience. While Edwards clearly affirms the place and use of the law in the life of the Christian, he never confuses justification with sanctification, though he affirms the impossibility of separating justification and sanctification. He shows how sanctification flows out of our justification.

In this Edwards again offers a warning to much of modern thinking, where justification emphasized at the expense of sanctification leads to antinomianism, and sanctification emphasized at the expense of justification leads to moralism. The great Tertullian wrote, "Just as Christ was crucified between two thieves, so the doctrine of justification is ever crucified between two opposite errors." The errors to which Tertullian referred, and which steal the gospel from the experience of the believer, are "legalism" and "antinomianism," or, as we would better describe them today, "moralism" and "relativism." Both are destructive of the Christian life, and both are seductive in their own ways. The moralist will tend to emphasize truth without grace, or imply that we must obey truth in order to be saved. The relativist will emphasize grace without truth, implying that we are all accepted by God, and arguing that everyone has to decide which "truth" is right for him. Edwards shows us afresh that truth without grace is not really truth, and that grace without truth is not really grace.

In the second of the sermons included here, "Hope and Comfort Usually Follow Genuine Humiliation and Repentance," Edwards carries on this theme by reminding us that the great reality with which we struggle is sin. Many are unaware of the seriousness, depth, and power of sin, which is why the idea of the sacrifice of Christ and the free grace of God has such little effect upon them. Edwards brings us a healthy dose of exposition of the law and offers a powerful vision of the offended holiness of God, which serve to bring us to the reality of the conviction of sin. For many of us, who hold rather too high a view of ourselves, this will be a helpful corrective.

Others, however, have an overwhelming sense of their own inadequacy and see only their failings, and to these Edwards brings the sweetness of the Christian experience of God's comfort. He reminds us that when we come to the gospel, there is repentance and reliance upon Christ.

The biblical repentance to which Edwards draws us is marked out by its all-encompassing nature. We repent not only of our sins but also of our righteousness, as we see the utter unacceptability of even our best deeds. By resting in Christ, by which we see ourselves as completely accepted by him, his record becomes ours, and our record is imputed to him. His blessings and the reward of his sacrifice become ours, and our sin is imputed to him. The consequence of this is an intense humility in our lives, and with it a blessing of comfort and sense of pardon. Paradoxically, we discover that the more sinful we see ourselves, the more radical appears the nature of the grace of God, and the sweeter the fruit of repentance becomes in our lives. Genuine repentance is brought about, ultimately, neither by the fear of consequences nor by the fear of rejection, but as a ministry of the Holy Spirit, who gives to us a deep conviction of the mercy of God.

Many people fail to recognize the nature of God's holiness, and so they also fail to appreciate the depth of human sin; thus they never fully learn to rejoice in the great grace of God. Others fail to appreciate the total and permanent nature of God's acceptance of his people by the work of Christ upon the cross and so live lives of fear. Edwards guides us to the understanding that, the more you realize the reality of your sinful nature, the more you are led to appreciate the enormity of the grace of God, and the more you are driven to find your assurance not in your works of righteousness, but rather in the grace of Christ. The gospel creates the only kind of grief over sin that is clean and does not crush, for it always points to Christ's dying for the believer, and thus always assures the Christian that Christ will never abandon or fail. The sight of Christ dying for us is at once the very thing that convicts us to be holy and yet assures us, at the same time, that we are unfailingly loved. For at the same time that the cross reminds us that Christ died for us, it also convicts our consciences to seek to be holy out of gratitude.

The third of the sermons in our selection is "The Preciousness of Time." In this address we are reminded not only of the very practical nature of our faith—that it has to be worked out in the details of life—but also of the intimate and necessary inseparability of the mind and the soul in the whole process of sanctification. To be holy is not simply to do great and noble acts. Holiness is not just about what we "do" any more than it is about the way we "feel." In an age of activism that is coupled with a curious spiritualism that is often more interested in feeling than in conviction, Edwards offers us a helpful and necessary corrective. He shows us in this sermon that we do need to think in order to be holy. He challenges the idea that holiness is either a matter of emotion or of action. Instead he reminds us of the biblical conjoining of mind and soul. He stresses the fact of our accountability before God, which has to be recognized and then acted upon. Edwards viewed the mind as the palace of faith, and knowledge was "the soil in which the Spirit planted the seed of regeneration in the soul." He addressed the mind in order that the soul should be blessed. This corrective to the culture of our generation reminds us that we cannot devalue Christian content in worship, education, or preaching without incurring a high cost. Already there seems to be little distinction between Christians and non-Christians in the ways they think or believe, or, indeed, in how they live.

Christian assurance cannot be found by looking at the transformed life, for that may be a life often lived more by law and fear than by grace and repentance. Nonetheless, the importance of transformation is that it is an evidence of the work of God's Spirit. Edwards always brings us a healthy reminder that the Holy Spirit bears fruit in every part of the Christian life.[2] He breaks down the artificial barriers erected between what is sacred and what is secular, forcing the believer to take seriously the call to devote the whole of his life, and every part of life, to the service of God as a fruit of union with Christ. Edwards knew and taught that we will grow in intimacy with Christ only when we live out a union with Christ.

There can hardly be a subject of more importance for the followers of Jesus Christ today than that of sanctification. In these pluralistic, relativistic, and "tolerant" times, many Christians have begun to dance to the piper of postmodernism and have lost sight of our calling to follow the apostle Paul in pressing on in holiness in the Lord. The sermons by Jonathan Edwards included in this volume can

2. For Edwards on the role of the Spirit in Christian growth, see volume 1 in this series, *Growing in God's Spirit* (Phillipsburg, N.J.: P&R, 2003).

provide a healthy and encouraging corrective to our faltering faith, and lead us to heights of holiness, joy, and powerful living that can bring renewal to our lives, our churches, and our culture.

Robert M. Norris
Senior Pastor
Fourth Presbyterian Church
Bethesda, Maryland

❖ *Part 1* ❖

THE CHARACTER
OF PAUL AN EXAMPLE
TO THE CHRISTIANS

❖ *Chapter 1* ❖

A CALL TO IMITATE

Edwards shows that God has been pleased to give us many examples to follow in pursuing holiness in the Lord. God himself is our supreme example, especially as manifested in Jesus Christ. But that particular example has some limitations, as Edwards explains. So God calls us in his Word to imitate others like ourselves, sinful human beings who have learned how to pursue holiness, and from whom we have much to learn. Primary among these, Edwards argues, is the apostle Paul.

❖

PHILIPPIANS 3:17
Brethren, be followers together of me, and mark them which walk so as ye have us for an ensample.

The apostle in the foregoing part of the chapter had been telling how he counted all things but loss for the excellency of the knowledge of Christ Jesus, and in the text he urges that his example should be followed.

He does this in two ways.

1. He exhorts the Philippian Christians to follow his example. "Brethren, be followers together of me." He

exhorts them to be followers of him *together*; that is, that they should all follow his example with one heart and soul, all agreeing in it, and that all, as much as in them lay, should help and assist each other in it.

2. That they should take particular notice of others that did so, and put peculiar honor on them; which is implied in the expression in the latter part of the verse, "mark them which walk so as ye have us for an ensample."

CHRIST OUR GREAT EXAMPLE

We ought to follow the good examples of the apostle Paul. We are to consider that the apostle did not say this of himself from an ambitious spirit, from a desire of being set up as a pattern and eyed and imitated as an example to other Christians. His writings are not of any private interpretation, but he spake as he was moved by the Holy Ghost. The Holy Ghost directed that the good examples of the apostle Paul should be noticed by other Christians and imitated. And we are also to consider that this is not a command to the Philippians only, to whom the epistle was more immediately directed, but to all those for whose use this epistle was written, for all Christians to the end of the world. For though God so ordered it that the epistles of the apostles were mostly written on particular occasions and directed to particular churches, yet they were written to be of universal use. And those occasions were so ordered in the wisdom of Divine Providence that they are a part of that infallible rule of faith and manners which God has given to the Christian church to be their rule in all ages. And the precepts that we find in those epistles are no more to be regarded as precepts intended only for those to whom the epistle was sent, than the Ten Commandments that were spoken from Mount Sinai to the children of Israel are to be regarded as commands intended only for that people. And when we are directed to follow the good examples of the apostle Paul by the Holy Ghost, it is not merely as we are to imitate whatever we see that is good in anyone, let him be who he may. But there are spiritual obligations that lie on Christians to follow the good examples of the great apostle. And it hath pleased the Holy Ghost in an especial manner to set up the apostle Paul not only as a teacher of the Christian church, but as a pattern to other Christians.

The greatest example of all that is set before us in the Scripture to imitate is the example of Jesus Christ, which he set us in his human nature and when in his state of humiliation. This is presented to us not only as a great pattern, but as a perfect rule. And the example of no man is set forth as our rule but the example of Christ. We are commanded to follow the examples which God himself set us, or the acts of the divine nature: "Be ye therefore followers of God, as dear children" (Eph. 5:1). And: "Be ye therefore perfect, even as your Father which is in heaven is perfect" (Matt. 5:48).

But the example of Christ Jesus when he was on earth is more especially our pattern. For, though the acts of the divine nature have the highest possible perfection, and though his inimitable perfection is our best example, yet God is so much above us, his nature so infinitely different from ours, that it is not possible that his acts should be so accommodated to our nature and circumstances as to be an example of so great and general use as the perfect example in our nature which Christ has set us. Christ, though a divine person, was man as we are men; and not only so, but he was, in many respects, a partaker of our circumstances. He dwelt among men. He depended on food and raiment and such outward supports of life as we do. He was subject to the changes of time and the afflictions and calamities of this evil world, and to abuse from men's corruptions, and to the same law and rule that we are; he used the same ordinances, and had many of our trials, and greater trials than we. So that Christ's example is chiefly offered in Scripture for our imitation.

OTHER EXAMPLES FROM SCRIPTURE

But yet the example of some that are fallen creatures, as we are, may in some respects be more accommodated to our circumstances and more fitted for our instruction than the example of Jesus Christ. For though he became a man as we are, and was like us, and was in our circumstances in so many respects, yet in other things there was a vast differ-ence. He was the head of the church, and we are the mem-bers. He is Lord of all; we are his subjects and disciples. And we need an example that shall teach and direct us how to behave toward Christ our Lord and head. And this we may have better in some that have Christ for their Lord as well as we, than in Christ himself.

But the greatest difference lies in this: that Christ had no sin, and we all are sinful creatures, all carry about with us a body of sin and death. It is said that Christ was made like us in all things, sin only excepted. But this was excepted, and therefore there were many things required of us of which Christ could not give us an example, such as repentance for sin, brokenness of spirit for sin, mortification of lust, warring against sin. And the excellent example of some that are naturally as sinful as we has this advantage: that we may regard it as the example of those who were naturally every way in our circumstances, and labored under the same natural difficulties and the same opposition of heart to that which is good, as ourselves; which tends to engage us to give more heed to their example, and the more to encourage and animate us to strive to follow it.

And therefore we find that the Scripture does not only recommend the example of Christ, but does also exhibit some mere men, that are of like passions with ourselves, as patterns for us to follow.

Old Testament saints

So it exhibits the eminent saints of the Old Testament, of whom we read in the Scripture that they inherit the promises: "That ye be not slothful, but followers of them who through faith and patience inherit the promises" (Heb. 6:12). In the eleventh chapter of Hebrews, a great number of eminent saints are mentioned as patterns for us to follow. Abraham is in a particular manner set forth as an example in his faith and as the pattern of believers: "And the father of circumcision to them that are not of the circumcision only, but who also walk in the steps of that faith of our father Abraham, which he had, being yet uncircumcised" (Rom. 4:12).

And so the prophets of the Old Testament are also recommended as patterns: "Take, my brethren, the prophets, who have spoken in the name of the Lord, for an example of suffering affliction, and of patience" (James 5:10).

New Testament saints

And so, eminently holy men under the New Testament, apostles and others, that God sent forth to preach the gospel, are also examples for Christians to follow: "Remember them that have the rule over you, who have spoken to you the Word of God; whose faith follow, considering the end of their conversation" (Heb. 13:7).

PAUL OUR PRIMARY EXAMPLE

But of all mere men, no one is so often particularly set forth in the Scripture as a pattern for Christians to follow as the apostle Paul. Our observing his holy conversation as our example is not only insisted on in our text, but also in 1 Corinthians 4:16: "Wherefore I beseech you, be ye followers of me." And 1 Corinthians 11:1: "Be ye followers of me as I also am of Christ." And 1 Thessalonians 1:6, where the apostle commends the Christian Thessalonians for imitating his example: "and ye became followers of us." And 2 Thessalonians 3:7, where he insists on this as their duty: "For yourselves know how ye ought to follow us."

For the more full treatment of this subject I shall:

I. Particularly mention many of the good examples of the apostle Paul that we ought to imitate, which I shall treat of not merely as a doctrine, but also in the way of application.

II. I shall show under what strict obligation we are to follow the good examples of this apostle.

And that I may be more distinct, I shall:

1. Mention those things that respect his watchfulness for the good of his own soul.

2. Those virtues in him that more immediately respected God and Christ.

3. Those that more immediately respect men.

4. Those that were exercised in his behavior both toward God and man.

STUDY QUESTIONS

1. From this introduction to Edwards's call to imitate the apostle Paul we might get the idea that believers learn the life of faith, at least in part, from observing and following the examples of others. Has this been true in your experience? Who are some people who have served as examples to you in your walk with the Lord? What have you learned from them?

2. Of course, Edwards insists that Christ is our supreme example. What should we expect to learn from imitating the Lord Jesus? What are the limitations in his example?

3. Edwards mentions Old Testament and New Testament saints as good examples for us to follow. Let's see if that's been true in your experience. List one or two saints from each Testament, and summarize how their example has been helpful to you:

a. Old Testament saints:
b. New Testament saints:

4. Review the four areas of Paul's example that Edwards plans to discuss (right at the end of this chapter). In which of these areas do you particularly sense a need for Paul's example to help you in your walk with the Lord? Explain.

5. What do you hope to gain from this study of the pursuit of holiness in the Lord? What are your goals? Is there someone you can enlist to pray with and for you as you undertake this study?

❖ Chapter 2 ❖

SEEKING THE GOOD
OF OUR SOULS (I)

*Edwards holds out the example of the apostle Paul as one we ought to
follow, first, in seeking the salvation of the Lord—and assurance of
salvation with it—and, second, in seeking to grow in salvation. Once
brought to his senses, convicted, and called to submit to Jesus, Paul
allowed nothing to stand in the way of his coming to faith in Christ,
and after his conversion he was even more diligent to gain the full
prize of salvation. Edwards continuously refers to Jesus' teaching in
Matthew 11:12 to show Paul's "violence" in seeking the kingdom and
salvation of God. He challenges us to follow Paul's example.*

We ought to follow the good example that the apostle
Paul has set us in his seeking the good of his own soul.

WITH RESPECT TO SALVATION

First. We should follow him in his earnestness in seeking his own salvation. He was not careless and indifferent
in this matter; but the kingdom of heaven suffered violence

from him. He did not halt between two opinions, or seek with a wavering, unsteady mind, but with the most full determination and strong resolution. He resolved, if it could by any means be possible, that he would attain to the resurrection of the dead. He does not say that he was determined to attain it, if he could, by means that were not costly or difficult, or by laboring for it a little time, or only now and then, or without any great degree of suffering, or without great loss in his temporal interest. But if by *any* means he could do it, he would, let the means be easy or difficult. Let it be a short labor and trial, or a long one; let the cross be light or heavy; it was all one to his resolution. Let the requisite means be what they would, if it were possible, he would attain it.

He did not hesitate at worldly losses, for he tells us that he readily suffered the loss of all things that he might win Christ and be found in him, and in his righteousness (Phil. 3:8–9). It was not with him as it was with the young man who came kneeling to Christ to inquire of him what he should do to inherit eternal life, and when Christ said, "Go and sell all that thou hast and give to the poor," he went away sorrowful. He was not willing to part with all. If Christ had bid him sell half, it may be he would have complied with it. He had a great desire to secure salvation. But the apostle Paul did not content himself with wishing. He resolved, if it were possible, that he would obtain it. And when it was needful that he should lose worldly good, or when any great suffering was in his way, it was no cause of hesitation to him. He had been in very comfortable and honorable circumstances among the Jews. He had received the best education that was to be had among them, being brought up at the feet of Gamaliel, and was regarded as a very learned young man. His own nation, the Jews, had a high esteem of him, and he was esteemed for his moral and religious qualifications among them. But when he could not hold the outward benefit of these things and win Christ, he despised them totally; he parted with all his credit and honor. He made nothing of them, that he might win Christ.

And instead of being honored and loved and living in credit, as before among his own nation, he made himself the object of their universal hatred. He lost all, and the Jews hated him and persecuted him everywhere. And when great sufferings were in the way, he willingly made himself conformable to Christ's death, that he might have a part in his resurrection. He parted with his honor, his ease, his former friends and former acquaintances, his worldly goods, and everything else, and plunged himself into a state of extreme labor, contempt, and suffering; and in this way he sought the kingdom of heaven. He acted in this matter very much as one who is running a race for some great prize, who makes running his great and only business, till he has reached the end of the race, and strains every nerve and sinew, and suffers nothing to divert him, and will not stand to listen to what anyone says to him, but presses forward. Or as a man who is engaged in battle, sword in hand, with strong and violent enemies that seek his life, who exerts himself to his utmost, as for his life: "I therefore so run, not as uncertainly; so fight I, not as one that beateth the air" (1 Cor. 9:26). When fleshly appetites stood in the way, however importunate they were, he utterly denied them and renounced them; they were no impediment in the way of his thorough pursuit of salvation. He would not be subject to the appetites of his body, but made them subject to his soul: "I keep under my body, and bring it into subjection" (1 Cor. 9:27).

Probably there never was a soldier, when he bore his part in storming a city, who acted with greater resolution and violence, as it were forcing his way through all that opposed him, than the apostle Paul in seeking the kingdom of heaven. We have not only his own word for it; the history we have of his life, written by St. Luke, shows the same. Now those who seek their salvation ought to follow this example. Persons who are concerned for their salvation sometimes inquire what they shall do. Let them do as did the apostle Paul; seek salvation in the way he did, with the like violence and resolution. Those who make this inquiry, who are somewhat anxious year after year and complain that they have not obtained any comfort, would do well to ask themselves whether they seek salvation in any measure in this way, with that resolution and violence of which he set them an example. Alas, are they not very far from it? Can it in any proper sense be said that the kingdom of heaven suffers violence at their hands?

WITH RESPECT TO THE PRIZE OF SALVATION

Second. The apostle did not only thus earnestly seek salvation before his conversion and hope, but afterwards also. What he says in the third chapter of Philippians of his suffering the loss of all things that he might be found in Christ, and its being the one thing that he did to seek salvation; and also what he says of his so running as not in vain, but as resolving to win the prize of salvation, and keeping under his body that he might not be a castaway; were long after his conviction, and after he had renounced all hope of his own good estate by nature. If being a convinced sinner excuses a man from seeking salvation any more, or makes it reasonable that he should cease his earnest care and labor for it, certainly the apostle might have been excused when he had not only already attained true grace, but such eminent degrees of it. To see one of the most eminent saints who ever lived, if not the most eminent of all, so exceedingly engaged in seeking his own salvation, ought forever to put to shame those who are a thousand degrees below him and are but mere infants to him, if they have any grace at all; who yet excuse themselves from using any violence after the kingdom of heaven now because they have attained already; who free themselves from the burden of going on earnestly to seek salvation with this, that they have finished the work, they have obtained a hope.

The apostle, as eminent as he was, did not say within himself, "I am converted, and so am sure of salvation.

Christ has promised it me; why need I labor any more to secure it? Yea, I am not only converted, but I have obtained great degrees of grace." But still he is violent after salvation. He did not keep looking back on the extraordinary discoveries he enjoyed at his first conversion, and the past great experience he had from time to time. He did not content himself with the thought that he possessed the most wonderful testimonies of God's favor and of the love of Christ already, that ever any enjoyed, even to his being caught up to the third heavens; but he forgot the things that were behind. He acted as though he did not consider that he had yet attained an interest in Christ: "If by any means I might attain unto the resurrection of the dead: not as though I had already attained, either were already perfect; but I follow after, if that I may apprehend that for which I am apprehended of Christ Jesus. Brethren, I count not myself to have apprehended; but this one thing I do, forgetting those things which are behind, and reaching forth to those things which are before, I press toward the mark for the prize of the high calling of God in Christ Jesus" (Phil. 3:11–14). The apostle still sought that he might win Christ and his righteousness and attain to his resurrection, not as though he had attained it already, or had already obtained a title to the crown. And this is especially the thing in which he calls on us to imitate his example in the text. It was not because Paul was at a loss whether he was truly converted, or not that he was still so earnest in seeking salvation. He not only thought that he was converted and should go to heaven when he died, but he knew and spoke particularly about it in this very epistle, in the twenty-first verse of the first chapter: "For me to live is Christ, but to die is gain." And in the foregoing verse he says, "According to my earnest expectation and my hope, that in nothing I shall be ashamed, but that with all boldness, as always, so now also Christ shall be magnified in my body, whether it be by life or by death" (Phil. 1:20).

The apostle knew that, though he was converted, yet there remained a great work that he must do in order to his salvation. There was a narrow way to eternal glory, through which he must pass, and never could come to heaven in any other way. He knew it was absolutely necessary for him earnestly to seek salvation still; he knew there was no going to heaven in a slothful way. And therefore he did not seek salvation the less earnestly, for his having hope and assurance, but a great deal more. We nowhere read so much of his earnestness and violence for the kingdom of heaven before he was converted, as afterwards. The apostle's hope was not of a nature to make him slothful; it had a contrary effect. The assurance he had of victory, together with the necessity there was of fighting, engaged him to fight not as one who beat the air, but as one who wrestled with principalities and powers. Now this example the apostle does especially insist upon in the text that we ought to follow. And this should induce all present who think themselves converted to inquire whether they seek salvation never the less earnestly because they think it is well with them, and that they are now sure of heaven. Most certainly if the apostle was in the right way of acting, we in this place are generally in the wrong. For nothing is more apparent than that it is not thus with the generality of professors here, but that it is a common thing after they think they are safe to be far less diligent and earnest in religion than before.

STUDY QUESTIONS

1. Edwards talks about the "violence" with which Paul sought to lay hold on the kingdom and salvation of God (Matt. 11:12). What are some of the things he mentions as examples of that "violence"?

2. Paul was more diligent *after* his conversion about gaining the salvation of the Lord than he was *before*. Before becoming a Christian he was violent against the Lord and his church. Only Christ's violent interruption of Paul's raging brought him to salvation on the road to Damascus (Acts 9). Would you describe your own pursuit of salvation, and of holiness in the Lord, as "violent"? Why or why not?

3. Summarize the price Paul had to pay for gaining the salvation of the Lord. Do you think that any of these things are obstacles for people today? Which?

4. In the last paragraph of this chapter Edwards unfavorably compared his hearers with the apostle Paul in this matter of seeking the salvation of the Lord. Do you think his assessment of the people in his own day (note

that he included himself) is still valid today? Explain your answer.

5. Suppose you were to begin becoming more "violent" in the pursuit of holiness and the salvation of God. What might that look like? Which aspects of Paul's example might you begin to make more a part of your own experience?

❖ Chapter 3 ❖

SEEKING THE GOOD
OF OUR SOULS (2)

Edwards continues to show ways in which Paul exercised great care for the good of his soul. Paul did not take his salvation for granted, but rather, worked hard in every way lest he be found disqualified from grace and subject to God's judgment. In so doing, he did not rely on his own righteousness, but sought the righteousness of Christ by faith. Finally, he was motivated in seeking the good of his soul by the reward of glory laid up for him in heaven.

WITH RESPECT TO ONGOING CAUTION

Third. The apostle did not only diligently seek heaven after he knew he was converted, but was earnestly cautious lest he should be damned, as appears by the passage already cited: "But I keep under my body and bring it into subjection, lest by any means, when I have preached to others, I myself should be a castaway" (1 Cor. 9:27). Here you see the apostle is very careful lest he should be a castaway, and denies his carnal appetites and mortifies his flesh for that reason. He did not say, "I am safe, and I am sure I shall never be lost; why need I take any further care respecting it?" Many think because they suppose themselves converted, and so safe, that they have nothing to do with the awful threatenings of God's Word, and those terrible denunciations of damnation that are contained in it. When they hear them, they hear them as things which belong only to others, and not at all to themselves, as though there were no application of what is revealed in the Scripture respecting hell, to the godly. And therefore, when they hear awakening sermons about the awful things that God has threatened to the wicked, they do not hear them for themselves, but only for others.

But it was not thus with the holy apostle, who certainly was as safe from hell and as far from a damnable state as any of us. He looked upon himself as still nearly concerned in God's threatenings of eternal damnation, notwithstanding all his hope and all his eminent holiness, and therefore gave great diligence that he might avoid eternal damnation. For he considered that eternal misery was as certainly connected with a wicked life as ever it was, and that it was absolutely necessary that he should still keep under his body and bring it into subjection, in order that he might not be damned; because indulging the lusts of the body and being damned were more surely connected together. The apostle knew that this conditional proposition was true concerning him, as ever it was: "If I live wickedly, or do not live in a way of universal obedience to God's commands, I shall certainly be a castaway."

This is evident, because the apostle mentions a proposition of this nature concerning himself in that very chapter where he says he kept under his body lest he should be a castaway: "For though I preach the gospel, I have nothing to glory of, for necessity is laid upon me; yea, woe is unto me if I preach not the gospel" (1 Cor. 9:16). What necessity was there upon the apostle to preach the gospel, though God had commanded him, for he was already converted and was safe; and if he had neglected to preach the gospel, how could he have perished after he was converted? But yet this conditional proposition was still true; if he did not live a life of obedience to God, woe would be to him; woe to him, if he did not preach the gospel. The connection still held. It is impossible a man should go anywhere else than to hell in a way of disobedience to God. And therefore he deemed it necessary for him to preach the gospel on that account, and on the same account he deemed it necessary to keep under his body, lest he should be a castaway. The connection between a wicked life and damnation is so certain that, if a man lives a wicked life, it proves that all his supposed experiences are nothing. If a man at the last day be found a worker of iniquity, nothing else will be inquired of about him. Let him pretend what he will, Christ will say to him and all others like him, "Depart from me, I know you not, ye that work iniquity" (Matt. 7:23). And God has revealed these threatenings and this connection not only to deter wicked men, but also godly men, from sin. And though God will keep men who are converted from damnation, yet this is the means by which he will keep them from it; namely, he will keep them from a wicked life. And though he will keep them from a wicked life, yet this is one means by which he will keep them from it; namely, by their own caution to avoid damnation, and by his threatenings of damnation if they should live a wicked life.

We have another remarkable instance in Job, who was an eminently holy man, yet avoided sin with the utmost care because he would avoid destruction from God (Job 31). Surely we have as much cause to be cautious that we do not expose ourselves to destruction from God, as holy Job had. We have not a greater stock of goodness than he. The apostle directs Christians to work out their own salvation with fear and trembling (Phil. 2:12). And it is spoken of as the character of a true saint that he trembles at God's Word (Isa. 66:2), which is to tremble especially at the awful threatenings of it, as Job did. Whereas the manner of many now is, whenever they think they are converted, to throw by those threatenings of God's Word as if they had no more to do with them, because they suppose they are converted and out of danger. Christ gave his disciples, even those of them who were converted, as well as others, directions to strive for salvation; because broad was the way that leads to destruction, and men are so apt to walk in that way and be damned: "Enter ye in at the strait gate; for wide is the gate, and broad is the way, that leadeth to destruction, and many there be which go in thereat; because strait is the gate, and narrow is the way that leadeth unto life, and few there be that find it" (Matt. 7:13–14).

With Respect to the Question of Righteousness

Fourth. The apostle did not seek salvation by his own righteousness. Though his sufferings were so very great, his labors so exceedingly abundant, yet he never accounted them as righteousness. He trod it under his feet as utterly insufficient to recommend him to God. He gave diligence that he might be found in Christ, not having on his own righteousness, which is of God, through faith, as in the foregoing part of the chapter from which the text is taken, beginning with the fourth verse:

> Though I might also have confidence in the flesh. If any other man thinketh he hath whereof he might trust in the flesh, I more; circumcised the eighth day, of the stock of Israel, of the tribe of Benjamin, an Hebrew of the Hebrews; as touching the law, a Pharisee; concerning zeal, persecuting the church; touching the righteousness which is in the law, blameless. But what things were gain to me, those I counted loss for Christ. Yea, doubtless, and I count all things but loss for the excellency of the knowledge of Christ Jesus, my Lord; for whom I have suffered the loss of all things, and do count them but dung, that I may win Christ, and be found in him, not having on mine own righteousness, which is of the law, but that which is through the faith of Christ, the righ-

teousness which is of God by faith; that I may know him, and the power of his resurrection, and the fellowship of his sufferings, being made conformable unto his death; if by any means I might attain unto the resurrection of the dead. Not as though I had already attained, either were already perfect; but I follow after, if that I may apprehend that for which also I am apprehended of Christ Jesus. (Phil. 3:4–12)

WITH RESPECT TO LOOKING FOR THE REWARD

Fifth. In those earnest labors which he performed, he had respect to the recompense of the reward. He did it for an incorruptible crown (1 Cor. 9:25). He sought a high degree of glory, for he knew the more he labored the more he should be rewarded, as appears from what he tells the Corinthians: "He that soweth sparingly, shall reap also sparingly; and he that soweth bountifully, shall also reap bountifully" (2 Cor. 9:6). And, "Every man shall receive his own reward, according to his own labor" (1 Cor. 3:8). That he had respect to that crown of glory which his Master had promised, in those great labors and sufferings, is evident from what he says to Timothy, a little before his death: "I have fought a good fight, I have finished my course, I have kept the faith; henceforth there is laid up for me a crown of righteousness, which the Lord, the righteous Judge, shall give me at that day; and not to me only, but unto all them also that love his appearing" (2 Tim. 4:7–8).

All Christians should follow his example in this also; they should not content themselves with the thought that they have goodness enough to carry them to heaven, but should earnestly seek high degrees of glory; for the higher degrees of glory are promised to extraordinary labors for God, for no other reason but that we should seek them.

STUDY QUESTIONS

1. This is a difficult section, because, if we do not read it carefully, we might get the impression that Edwards believed we are saved by works. But this is not what he taught. Rather, what he believed is more along these lines: We are not saved *by* works, but we are not saved *without* them. What is the difference in these two statements? How is it apparent from this chapter that this is, in fact, what Edwards believed?

2. Edwards insisted that it is not enough simply to say: "I've professed faith in Christ, and I know I'm going to heaven. There's nothing else to worry about." From what you see in this chapter, how would Edwards respond to such a claim?

3. What does Edwards mean—indeed, what was Paul talking about—when he teaches us to seek "the righteousness which is of God by faith"? How would you counsel someone to go about seeking that righteousness? What would the attainment of that righteousness look like in someone's life? Why is it important to seek such righteousness?

4. Paul was motivated to seek the good of his soul by concentrating on the rewards laid up for him in heaven. He wanted the greatest amount of glory, the most brilliant crown, and therefore he worked so hard both to grow in the Lord and to do the work appointed to him. Is it right for us to be so motivated? What does it mean to seek crowns of glory? According to Revelation 4:9–10, what will we do with those crowns of glory? What does that mean? Does that give us any greater incentive to seek such rewards?

5. Summarize the five ways we have seen that Paul is an example for us of seeking the good of our souls as we pursue holiness in the Lord:

   a. with respect to salvation:
   b. with respect to the prize of salvation:
   c. with respect to ongoing caution:
   d. with respect to the question of righteousness:
   e. with respect to looking for the reward:

   Now think carefully about each of your five summaries. Using a scale of 1 to 10, with 10 being the highest rating, to what extent would you say that your life is characterized by these five ways of pursuing holiness in the Lord? Where do you most need to begin seeking improvement?

❈ *Chapter 4* ❈

THE VIRTUES OF PAUL TOWARD GOD

Edwards enumerates seven virtues in which Paul excelled toward God. Every Christian should want to follow the example of Paul's strength of faith, love to Christ, confidence in the gospel, contempt of the world, abundance of prayer and praise, contentment in the Lord, and caution in giving an account of himself.

I proceed to mention some of the virtues of Paul that more immediately respect God and Christ, in which we ought to follow his example.

STRONG IN FAITH

First. He was strong in faith. It may be truly said of him that he lived by faith. His faith seemed to be even without the least appearance of diffidence or doubt in his words or actions, but all seemed to proclaim that he had God and Christ and the invisible world continually in view. Such a faith that was in continual exercise in him, he professes in

2 Corinthians 5:6–8: "Therefore we are always confident, knowing that while we are at home in the body, we are absent from the Lord. For we walk by faith, not by sight. We are confident, I say, and willing rather to be absent from the body, and to be present with the Lord."

Faith in things invisible

He always speaks of God and Christ and things invisible and future as if he certainly knew them, and then saw them as fully and certainly as we see any thing that is immediately before our bodily eyes. He spoke as though he certainly knew that God's promise of eternal life should be accomplished, and gives this as the reason why he labored so abundantly and endured all manner of temporal sufferings and death, and was always delivered unto death for Christ's sake: "For we which live are always delivered unto death for Jesus' sake, that the life also of Jesus might be made manifest in our mortal flesh" (2 Cor. 4:11).

Faith in the face of martyrdom

He speaks of his earnest expectation and hope of the fulfillment of God's promises. And a little before his death, when he was a prisoner, and when he knew that he was like to bear the trial of martyrdom, which is the greatest trial of faith, he expresses his faith in Christ in the strongest terms: "For the which cause I also suffer these things; nevertheless I am not ashamed, for I know whom I have believed, and am persuaded that he is able to keep that which I have committed unto him against that day" (2 Tim. 1:12).

Such an example may well make us ashamed; for how weak and unsteady is the faith of most Christians! If now and then there seems to be a lively exercise of faith, giving the person at that time a firm persuasion and confidence, yet how short are such exercises, how soon do they vanish! How often is faith shaken with one temptation; how often are the exercises of it interrupted with doubting, and how much is exhibited of a diffident, vibrating spirit! How little does our faith accomplish in times of trial; how often and how easily is our confidence in God shaken and interrupted, and how frequently does unbelief prevail! This is much to the dishonor of our Savior Jesus Christ, as well as very painful to us. What a happy and glorious lot it is to live such a life of faith as Paul lived! How far did he soar on the wings of his strong faith above those little difficulties that continually molest us and are ready to overcome us! Seeing we have such a blessed example set before us in the Scriptures, let it prompt us earnestly to seek that we may soar higher also.

LOVE TO CHRIST

Second. Another virtue in which we should follow his example is his great love to Christ. The Corinthians, who saw how the apostle acted, how he labored, and how he suffered, and could see no worldly motive, were astonished. They wondered what it was that so wonderfully influenced and actuated the man. The apostle says that he was a spectacle to the world. But this was the immediate principle that moved him: his strong, his intense love to his glorious Lord and Master.

The love of Christ constraining

This love constrained him so that he could do nothing else than strive and labor and seek for his salvation. This account he gives of it himself: "The love of Christ constraineth us" (2 Cor. 5:14). He had such a delight in the Lord Jesus Christ, and in the knowledge and contemplation of him, that, he tells us, he "counted all things but loss for the excellency of the knowledge of Christ Jesus" (Phil. 3:8). He speaks in very positive terms. He does not say merely that he hopes he loves Christ, so as to despise other things in comparison of the knowledge of him; but "yea, doubtless, I count all things but loss for the excellency of the knowledge of Christ Jesus, my Lord." And he assigns this reason why he even gloried in his sufferings for Christ's sake: because the love of God was shed abroad in his heart by the Holy Ghost (Rom. 5:5). This expression seems to imply that he sensibly felt that holy affection, sweetly and powerfully diffused in his soul, like some precious, fragrant ointment.

The love of Christ in suffering

And how does he triumph in his love to Christ in the midst of his sufferings! "Who shall separate us from the love of Christ? Shall tribulation, or distress, or persecution, or famine, or nakedness, or peril, or sword? As it is written, 'For thy sake we are killed all the day long; we are accounted as sheep for the slaughter.' Nay, in all these things we are more than conquerors, through him that hath loved us" (Rom. 8:35–37).

May not this make us ashamed of our cold, dead hearts that we hear so often of Christ, of his glorious excellencies and his wonderful love, with so little emotion, our hearts being very commonly frozen up like a clod of earth by worldly affections? And it may be that now and then with much difficulty we persuade ourselves to do a little or expend a little for the advancement of Christ's kingdom; and then are ready to boast of it, that we have done so nobly. Such superior examples as we have are enough to make us ever blush for our own attainments in the love of Christ, and to rouse us earnestly to follow after those who have gone so far beyond us.

NOT ASHAMED OF THE GOSPEL

Third. The apostle lived in a day when Christianity was greatly despised; yet he was not ashamed of the gospel of Christ. Christians were everywhere despised by the great men of the world. Almost all those who made any figure in the world—men in honorable stations, men of learning, men of wealth—despised Christianity, and accounted it a mean, contemptible thing to be a Christian, a follower and worshipper of a poor, crucified man. To be a Christian was regarded as what ruined a man's reputation. Christians were everywhere looked upon as fools and were derided and mocked. They were the meanest of mankind, the offscouring of the world. This was a great temptation to Christians to be ashamed of the gospel.

Paul greatly tempted to be ashamed

And the apostle Paul was more especially in such circumstances as exposed him to this temptation, for before he was a Christian, he was in great reputation among his own countrymen. He was esteemed a young man of more than ordinary proficiency in learning, and was a man of high distinction among the Pharisees, a class of men of the first standing among Jews. In times when religion is much despised, great men are more ready to be ashamed of it than others. Many of the great seem to think that to appear religious men would make them look little. They do not know how to comply with showing a devout spirit, a spirit of supreme love to God, and a strict regard to God's commands. But yet the apostle was not ashamed of the gospel of Christ anywhere, or before any person. He was not ashamed of it among his own countrymen, the Jews, or before their rulers and scribes and great men, but ever boldly professed it, and confronted them in their opposition. When he was at Athens, the chief seat of learning and of learned men in the world, though the learned men and philosophers there despised his doctrine and called him a babbler for preaching the gospel; yet he felt no shame, but boldly disputed with and confounded those great philosophers, and converted some of them. And when he came to Rome, the metropolis and mistress of the world, where resided the emperor and senators and the chief rulers of the world, he was not ashamed of the gospel there. He tells the Romans, "I am ready to preach the gospel to you that are at Rome also. For I am not ashamed of the gospel of Christ; for it is the power of God unto salvation to everyone that believeth" (Rom. 1:15–16).

Not ashamed in the face of derision

The apostle was greatly derided and despised for preaching a crucified Jesus: "We are made as the filth of the world, and are the offscouring of all things unto this day" (1 Cor. 4:13). And in the tenth verse he says, "We are fools for Christ's sake." They were everywhere accounted and called fools. Yet the apostle was so far from being ashamed of the crucified Jesus that he gloried in him above all things: "God forbid that I should glory, save in the cross of our Lord Jesus Christ" (Gal. 6:14).

Here is an example for us to follow if at any time we fall in among those who hold religion in contempt, and will despise us for our pretensions to religion, and will be ready to deride us for being so precise, and look upon us as fools; that we may not be ashamed of religion and yield to sinful compliances with vain and loose persons, lest we should appear singular, and be looked upon as ridiculous. Such a meanness of spirit possesses many persons, who are not worthy to be called Christians, and are such as Christ will be ashamed of when he comes in the glory of his Father with the holy angels.

CONTEMPT OF THE WORLD

Fourth. Another virtue in which we ought to follow the apostle is his contempt of the world, and his heavenly-mindedness.

Condemning the world's enjoyments

He condemned all the vain enjoyments of the world. He despised its riches: "I have coveted no man's silver, or gold, or apparel" (Acts 20:33). He despised the pleasures of the world: "I keep under my body" (1 Cor. 9:27). The apostle's pleasures were in the sufferings of his body instead of the gratification of his carnal appetites: "Therefore I take pleasure in infirmities, in reproaches, in necessities, in persecutions, in distresses, for Christ's sake" (2 Cor. 12:10). He despised the honors of the world: "Nor of men sought we glory; neither of you, nor yet of others" (1 Thess. 2:6). He declares that the world was crucified unto him, and he unto the world.

Seeking unseen things

These were not the things that the apostle sought, but the things that were above, that were out of sight to other men: "While we look not at the things which are seen, but at the things which are not seen" (2 Cor. 4:18). He longed greatly after heaven: "For we that are in this tabernacle do groan, being burdened; not for that we would be unclothed, but clothed upon, that mortality might be swallowed up in life" (2 Cor. 5:4). And he tells us that he knew no man after the flesh; that is, he did not look upon the men or things of this world, or regard them as related to the world, or as they respected the present life; but he considered all men and all things as they had relation to a spiritual nature and to another world.

In this the apostle acted as becomes a Christian; for Christians, those who are indeed so, are people who belong not to this world, and therefore it is very unbecoming in them to have their minds taken up about these things. The example of Paul may make all such persons ashamed who have their minds chiefly occupied about the things of the world, about gaining estates, or acquiring honors; and yet would be accounted fellow disciples with the apostle, partakers of the same labors, and fellow heirs of the same heavenly inheritance. And it should prompt us to strive for more indifference to this world, and for more heavenly-mindedness.

ABOUNDING IN PRAYER AND PRAISE

Fifth. We ought also to follow the example of the apostle in abounding in prayer and praise. He was very earnest and greatly engaged in those duties, and continued in them, as appears from many passages. Romans 1:8: "First, I thank my God through Jesus Christ for you all, that your faith is spoken of throughout the whole world. For God is my witness, whom I serve with my spirit in the gospel of his Son, that without ceasing I make mention of you always in my prayers." Ephesians 1:15–16: "Wherefore I also, after I heard of your faith in the Lord Jesus and love unto all the saints, cease not to give thanks for you, making mention of you in my prayers." Colossians 1:3: "We give thanks to God, and the Father of our Lord Jesus Christ, praying always for you." First Thessalonians 1:2–3: "We give thanks to God always for you all, making mention of you in our prayers; remembering without ceasing your work of faith and labor of love, and patience of hope in our Lord Jesus Christ, in the sight of God and our Father." And 3:9–10: "For what thanks can we render to God again for you, for all the joy wherewith we joy for your sakes before our God; night and day praying exceedingly, that we might see your face, and might perfect that which is lacking in your faith?" Second Timothy 1:3: "I thank God, whom I serve from my forefathers with a pure conscience, that without ceasing I have remembrance of thee in my prayers, night and day."

CONTENTMENT IN THE LORD

Sixth. We ought to follow him in his contentment under the allotments of Divine Providence. He was the subject of a vast variety of dispensations of Providence. He went through a great many changes, and was almost continually in suffering circumstances, sometimes in one respect, sometimes in another, and sometimes the subject of a great many kinds of suffering together. But yet he had attained to such a degree of submission to the will of God as to be contented in every condition, and under all dispensations toward him: "Not that I speak in respect of want, for I have learned in whatsoever state I am, therewith to be content. I know both how to be abased, and I know how to abound. Everywhere, and in all things, I am instructed both to be full and to be hungry, both to abound and to suffer need. I can do all things through Christ which strengtheneth me" (Phil. 4:11–13).

What a blessed temper and disposition of mind was this to which Paul had arrived; and how happy is that man of whom it can now be said with truth! He is, as it were, out of the reach of every evil. Nothing can touch him so as to disturb his rest, for he rests in everything that God orders.

CAUTION IN HIS ACCOUNTING OF HIMSELF

Seventh. We should follow the apostle in his great caution in giving an account of his experiences so as not to present more of himself in his words than men should see in his deeds. In 2 Corinthians 12 he gives somewhat of an account of how he had been favored with visions and revelations, and had been caught up to the third heavens. And in the sixth verse, intimating that he could relate more, he breaks off, and forbears to say anything further respecting his experience. And he gives the reason for it, namely, that he would avoid, in what he relates of himself, giving occasion for anyone to be disappointed in him, in expecting more from him by his own account of his experience and revelations than he should see or hear of him in his conversation. His words are, "For though I would desire to glory, I shall not be a fool; for I will say the truth; but now I forbear, lest any man should think of me above that which he seeth me to be, or that he heareth of me" (2 Cor. 12:6).

Some may wonder at this in such a man as the apostle, and may say, Why should a man so eminent in his conversation be so cautious in this matter? Why need he be afraid to declare all the extraordinary things that he had witnessed, since his life was so agreeable, so eminently answerable to his experience? But yet you see the apostle forbore upon this very account. He knew there was great need of caution in this matter. He knew that if, in giving an account of his extraordinary revelations, he should give rise to an expectation of too great things in his conversation, and should not live answerably to that expectation, it would greatly wound religion. He knew that his enemies would be ready to say presently, "Who is this? The man who gives so extraordinary an account of his visions and revelations, and peculiar tokens of God's favor to him; does he live no more conformably to it?" But if such a man as the apostle, so eminent in his life, was cautious in this respect, surely we have need to be cautious, who fail so much more in our example than he did, and in whose conversation the enemy may find so much more occasion to speak reproachfully of religion.

This teaches us that it would be better to refrain wholly from boasting of our experience than to represent ourselves as better than our deeds and conversation represent us. For men will compare one with the other. And if they do not see a correspondence between them, this will be much more to the dishonor of God than our account will be to his honor. Let Christians, therefore, be warned to be ever cautious in this respect, after the great example of the apostle.

STUDY QUESTIONS

1. See if you can summarize in a few words the seven virtues toward God that Edwards identified in the apostle Paul in this chapter:

   a. strength of faith:
   b. love to Christ:
   c. not ashamed of the Gospel:
   d. contempt of the world:
   e. abundance of prayer and praise:
   f. contentment in the Lord:
   g. caution in giving an account of himself:

2. Look at each of your summaries of the virtues above and, using a scale of 1 to 10, with 10 being the highest rating, assess the state of these virtues in your own life. Where is there room for you to improve in becoming more like the apostle Paul?

3. Think of the Christians you know—the people with whom you spend time in church and in various other Christian

activities. Do you sense that they think very much about the virtues Paul had toward God? Why or why not?

4. What is our responsibility to one another to promote improvement in these virtues? How might we begin to be more faithful in this?

5. Review the goals you set for this study at the end of chapter 1. Are you making any progress in attaining them?

❄ *Chapter 5* ❄

VIRTUES OF PAUL TOWARD MEN

Having discussed the virtues Paul demonstrated toward God, Edwards now examines those which he showed particularly toward his fellow human beings. Edwards shows that in his meekness, peaceableness, compassion, rejoicing with others, love of fellowship, and courtesy Paul is an example for believers to follow today.

I shall mention some of those virtues of the apostle that more immediately respected men, in which we ought to follow his example.

MEEKNESS

First. His meekness under abuses, and his love to his enemies. There were multitudes that hated him, but there is no appearance of his hating any. The greater part of the world where he went were his enemies. But he was the friend of everyone, and labored and prayed earnestly for the good of all. And when he was reproached and derided and buffeted, still it was with meekness and gentleness of spirit that he bore all, and wished well to them nonetheless, and sought their good: "Being reviled, we bless; being persecuted, we suffer it; being defamed, we entreat" (I Cor. 4:12–13).

In that period of his sufferings when he went up to Jerusalem and there was such an uproar about him, and the people were in so furious a rage against him, eagerly thirsting for his blood, he discovered no anger or ill will toward his persecutors. At that time when he was a prisoner through their malice and stood before king Agrippa, and Agrippa said, "Almost thou persuadest me to be a Christian," and his blood-thirsty enemies were standing by, he replied, "I would to God that not only thou, but also all that hear me this day, were both almost and altogether such as I am, except these bonds." He wished that his accusers, and those who had bound themselves with an oath that they would neither eat nor drink till they had killed him, had all of them as great privileges and as much of the favor of heaven as himself; and that they were altogether as he was, except his bonds and imprisonment, and those afflictions which they had brought upon him. He did not desire that they should be like him in that affliction, though it was the fruit of their own cruelty.

And when some of the Corinthians, whom he had instructed and converted from heathenism, had dealt ill by him, had hearkened to some false teachers who had been among them, who hated and reproached the apostle, he tells them, in 2 Corinthians 12:15, notwithstanding these abuses, that still he would very gladly spend and be spent for them, though the more abundantly he loved them, the less he should be loved by them. If they returned him no thanks for his love, but only ill will and ill treatment, still he stood ready to spend and be spent for them.

And though the apostle was so hated, and had suffered so many abuses from the unbelieving Jews, yet how does he express his love to them? He prayed earnestly for them: "Brethren, my heart's desire and prayer to God for Israel is, that they might be saved" (Rom. 10:1). And he went mourning for them. He went about with a heavy heart, and with continual grief and sorrow, from compassion for them, under the calamities of which they were the subjects; and he declares in the most solemn manner that he had so great desire for their salvation that he could find it in his heart to wish himself accursed from Christ for them, and to be offered up a sacrifice, if that might be a means of their salvation (Rom. 9:1–3). We are to understand it of a temporal curse. He could be willing to die an accursed death, and so be made a curse for a time, as Christ was, if that might be a means of salvation to them.

How are those reproved by this, who, when they are abused and suffer reproach or injury, have thereby indulged a spirit of hatred against their neighbor, a prejudice whereby they are always apt to entertain a distrust, and to seek and embrace opportunities against them, and to be sorry for their prosperity and glad at their disappointments.

PEACEABLENESS

Second. He delighted in peace. When any contention happened among Christians, he was exceedingly grieved by it, as when he heard of the contentions that broke out in the Corinthian church. He intimates to the Philippians how he should rejoice at their living in love and peace, and therefore earnestly entreats them that they should so live: "If there be therefore any consolation in Christ, if any comfort of love, if any fellowship of the Spirit, if any bowels and mercies, fulfill ye my joy, that ye be like-minded, having the same love, being of one accord, of one mind" (Phil. 2:1–2).

And he studied those things that should make for peace. To that end he yielded to everyone as much as possible in those things that were lawful, and complied with the weakness and humors of others oftentimes, for the sake of peace. He declares that though he was free from all men, yet he had made himself servant of all. To the Jews he became as a Jew; to them that were under the law, as under the law; to them that were without law, as without law; to the weak he became as weak. He rather chose to please others than himself, for the sake of peace and the good of their souls. "Even as I please all men in all things, not seeking mine own profit, but the profit of many, that they may be saved" (1 Cor. 10:33).

COMPASSION

Third. He was of a most tender, compassionate spirit toward any that were in affliction. He showed such a spirit especially in the case of the incestuous Corinthian. The crime was very great, and the fault of the church was great in suffering such wickedness among them, and this occasioned the apostle to write with some sharpness to them respecting it. But when the apostle perceived that his reproof was laid to heart by the Corinthian Christians, and that they repented and their hearts were filled with sorrow, though he rejoiced at it, yet he was so affected with their sorrow that his heart yearned toward them, and he was almost ready to repent that he had written so severely to them. He was full of concern about it, lest his former letter should have filled them with overmuch sorrow: "For though I made you sorry with a letter, I do not repent, though I did repent; for I perceive that the same epistle hath made you sorry, though it were but for a season" (2 Cor. 7:8). So he had compassion for the incestuous man, though he had been guilty of so vile a crime, and was greatly concerned that he should be comforted. Whenever any Christian suffered or was hurt, the apostle says he felt it and suffered himself: "Who is weak, and I am not weak? Who is offended, and I burn not?" (2 Cor. 11:29).

REJOICING WITH OTHERS

Fourth. He rejoiced at others' prosperity and joy. When he saw the soul of any comforted, the apostle was a sharer with him; his soul was comforted also. When he saw any Christian refreshed in his spirit, his own spirit was refreshed: "Nevertheless, God that comforteth those that are cast down, comforted us by the coming of Titus; and not by his coming only, but by the consolation wherewith he was comforted in you, when he told us your earnest desire, your mourning, your fervent mind toward me, so that I rejoiced the more" (2 Cor. 7:6–7). And: "Therefore we were comforted in your comfort; yea, and exceedingly the more joyed we for the joy of Titus, because his spirit was refreshed by you all" (2 Cor. 7:13).

LOVE OF FELLOWSHIP

Fifth. He delighted in the fellowship of God's people. He longed after them when absent: "For God is my record how greatly I long after you in the bowels of Christ" (Phil. 1:8). And also: "Therefore, my brethren, dearly beloved and longed for, my joy and crown" (Phil 4:1). So also Romans 1:11–12: "For I long to see you, that I may impart unto you some spiritual gift, to the end ye may be established; that is, that I may be comforted together with you by the mutual faith both of you and me."

COURTESY

Sixth. He was truly courteous in his behavior toward others. Though he was so great a man and had so much honor put upon him of God, yet he was full of courtesy toward all men, rendering to all suitable respect. Thus when he was called before Jewish or heathen magistrates, he treated them with the honor and respect due to their places. When the Jews took him in the temple, though they behaved themselves more like devils than men, yet he addresses them in terms of high respect—"Men, brethren, and fathers, hear ye my defense"—calling the Jews his *brethren*, and saluting the elders and scribes with the title of *fathers*, though they were a body of infidels. So when he pleads his cause before Festus, a heathen governor, he gives him the title that belonged to him in his station, calling him "Most noble Festus."

His courtesy also appears in his salutations in his epistles. He is particularly careful to mention many persons, directing that his salutations should be given to them. Such a degree of courtesy, in so great a person as the apostle, reproves all those professing Christians, who, though far below him, are not courteous and respectful in their behavior to their neighbors, and especially to their superiors. Incivility is here reproved, and the too common neglect of Christians is reproved, who do not take strict care that their children are taught good manners and politeness, and brought up in a respectful and courteous behavior toward others.

STUDY QUESTIONS

1. Let's consider the virtues that Paul demonstrated toward other people with respect to how we see them in the church today. Among the list below, which virtues seem to

be particularly present, and which particularly lacking in your church?

a. meekness:
b. peaceableness:
c. compassion:
d. rejoicing with others:
e. love of fellowship:
f. courtesy:

2. How does your church endeavor deliberately to inculcate such virtues? For example, are they discussed in Bible study groups? Is there any accountability among members to improve in these virtues? How do you endeavor to improve in these virtues?

3. What about in your community? Which of these virtues appear to be most lacking in the community where your church is located? Do the churches have any responsibility here? Explain.

4. Suggest some ways in which Christians—say, members of a Bible study group or a Sunday school class—might help one another to improve in these virtues over time.

5. How might improvement in these virtues on the part of your church as a whole affect your witness in the larger community?

❊ *Chapter 6* ❊

THE VIRTUES OF PAUL TOWARD GOD AND MEN

The longest section of this sermon is given to an examination of those particular virtues characteristic of the apostle Paul which both honored God and redounded to the well-being of people because their focus was on the advancement of Christ's kingdom and the building of his church. Edwards mentions Paul's public-spiritedness, his diligence in doing good, his great skill in laboring for the gospel, his willingness to forego lawful things, and his readiness to suffer.

I shall mention those virtues of the apostle that respected both God and men, in which we should imitate his example.

PUBLIC-SPIRITEDNESS

First. He was a man of a most public spirit; he was greatly concerned for the prosperity of Christ's kingdom and the good of his church. We see a great many men wholly engaged in pursuit of their worldly interests: many who are earnest in pursuit of their carnal pleasures, many who are eager in the pursuit of their honors, and many who are violent in the pursuit of gain; but we probably never saw any man more engaged to advance his estate, nor more taken up with his pleasures, nor more greedy of honor, than the apostle Paul was about the flourishing of Christ's kingdom and the good of the souls of men.

The things that grieve men are outward crosses: losses in estates, or falling under contempt, or bodily sufferings. But these things grieved not him. He made little account of them. The things that grieved him were those that hurt the interests of religion, and about those his tears were shed. Thus he was exceedingly grieved, and wept greatly, for the corruptions that had crept into the church of Corinth, which was the occasion of his writing his first epistle to them: "For out of much affliction and anguish of heart, I wrote unto you, with many tears" (2 Cor. 2:4). The things about which other men are jealous are their worldly advantages and pleasures. If these are threatened, their jealousy is excited, since they are above all things dear to them. But the things that kindled the apostle's jealousy were those that seemed to threaten the interests of religion and the good of the church: "For I am jealous over you with a godly jealousy; for I have espoused you to one husband, that I may present you as a chaste virgin to Christ. But I fear, lest by any means, as the serpent beguiled Eve through his subtlety, so your minds should be corrupted from the simplicity that is in Christ" (2 Cor. 11:2–3).

The things at which other men rejoice are their amass-
ing earthly treasures, their being advanced to honors, their
being possessed of outward pleasures and delights. But
these excited not the apostle's joy; but when he saw or
heard of anything by which the interests of religion were
promoted and the church of Christ prospered, he rejoiced,
as in 1 Thessalonians 1:3: "Remembering without ceasing
your work of faith and labor of love, and patience of hope
in our Lord Jesus Christ, in the sight of God and our
Father." And in 2:20: "Ye are our glory and joy." He
rejoiced at those things, however dear they cost him, how
much soever he lost by them in his temporal interest, if the
welfare of religion and the good of souls were promoted:
"Holding forth the word of life, that I may rejoice in the
day of Christ, that I have not run in vain, neither labored
in vain. Yea, and if I be offered upon the sacrifice and service of your faith, I joy and rejoice with you all" (Phil.
2:16–17). He rejoiced at the steadfastness of saints: "For
though I be absent in the flesh, yet am I with you in the
spirit, joying and beholding your order, and the steadfastness of your faith in Christ" (Col. 2:5). And he rejoiced at
the conviction of sinners, and in whatever tended to it. He
rejoiced at any good which was done, though by others, and
though it was done accidentally by his enemies:

> Some indeed preach Christ even of envy and strife; and
> some also of good will. The one preach Christ of con-
> tention, not sincerely, supposing to add affliction to my
> bonds. But the other of love, knowing that I am set for

the defense of the gospel. What then? Notwithstanding, every way, whether in pretense or in truth, Christ is preached; and I therein do rejoice, yea, and I will rejoice. (Phil. 1:15–18)

When the apostle heard anything of this nature, it was good news to him: "But now, when Timotheus came from you unto us, and brought us good tidings of your faith and charity, and that ye have good remembrance of us always, desiring greatly to see us, as we also you; therefore, brethren, we were comforted over you in all our affliction and distress by your faith" (1 Thess. 3:6–7). When he heard such tidings, his heart was wont to be enlarged in the praises of God: "We give thanks to God and the Father of our Lord Jesus Christ, praying always for you, since we heard of your faith in Christ Jesus, and of the love which ye have to all the saints" (Col 1:3–4). He was not only wont to praise God when he first heard such tidings, but as often as he thought of such things, they were so joyful to him that he readily praised God: "I thank my God upon every remembrance of you, always in every prayer of mine for you all making request with joy, for your fellowship in the gospel from the first day until now" (Phil. 1:3–5).

Let us compare ourselves with such an example, and examine how far we are of such a spirit. Let those on this occasion reflect upon themselves, whose hearts are chiefly engaged in their own private temporal concerns and are not much concerned respecting the interests of religion and the church of Christ, if they can obtain their private aims; who are greatly grieved when things go contrary to their worldly prosperity; who see religion, as it were, weltering in its blood, without much sorrow of heart. It may be that they will say, "It is greatly to be lamented that there is so much declension, and it is a sorrowful thing that sin so much prevails." But if we would look into their hearts, how cold and careless should we see them. Those words are words of course. They express themselves thus chiefly because they think it creditable to lament the decay of religion; but they are ten times as much concerned about other things as these—about their own private interest, or some secular affairs of the town. If anything seems to threaten their being disappointed in these things, how readily they are excited and alarmed; but how quiet and easy in their spirit, notwithstanding all the dark clouds that appear over the cause and kingdom of Christ, and the salvation of those around them! How quick and how high is their zeal against those, who, they think, unjustly oppose them in their temporal interests; but how low is their zeal, comparatively, against those things that are exceedingly pernicious of the interests of religion! If their own credit is touched, how they are awakened! But they can see the credit of religion wounded and bleeding and dying, with little hearty concern. Most men are of a private, narrow spirit. They are not of the spirit of the apostle Paul, nor of the psalmist, who preferred Jerusalem above his chief joy (Ps. 137:6).

DILIGENCE IN DOING GOOD

Second. We ought to follow the apostle in his diligent and laborious endeavors to do good. We see multitudes incessantly laboring and striving after the world; but not more than the apostle labored to advance the kingdom of his dear Master and the good of his fellow creatures. His work was very great, and attended with great difficulties and opposition; and his labor was answerably great. He labored abundantly more than any of the apostles: "I labored more abundantly than they all, yet not I, but the grace of God which was with me" (1 Cor. 15:10).

How great were the pains he took in preaching and in traveling from place to place over so great part of the world by sea and land—and probably for the most part on foot, when he traveled on land—instructing and converting the heathen; disputing with gainsayers and heathen and Jews and heretics; strenuously opposing and fighting against the enemies of the church of Christ, wrestling not with flesh and blood, but against principalities and powers, against the rulers of the darkness of this world, against spiritual wickedness in high places; acting the part of a good soldier, as one that goes a warfare, putting on Christ and using the whole armor of God; laboring to establish and confirm and build up the saints, reclaiming those who were wandering, delivering those who were ensnared, enlightening the dark, comforting the disconsolate, and succoring the tempted; rectifying disorders that had happened in churches, exercising ecclesiastical discipline toward offenders and admonishing the saints of the covenant of grace; opening and applying the Scriptures; ordaining persons and giving them directions, and assisting those who were ordained; and writing epistles and sending messengers to one and another part of the church of Christ! He had the care of the churches lying continually upon him: "Besides those things that are without, that which cometh upon me daily, the care of all the churches" (2 Cor. 11:28). These things occasioned him to be continually engaged in earnest labor. He continued in it day and night, sometimes almost the whole night, preaching and admonishing, as appears by Acts 20:7, 11: "And upon the first day of the week, when the disciples came together to break bread, Paul preached unto them, ready to depart on the morrow, and continued his speech until midnight. . . . When he therefore was come again, and had broken bread and eaten, and talked a long while, even till break of day, so he departed." And he did all freely, without any view to any temporal gain. He tells the Corinthians that he would gladly spend and be spent for them.

Besides his laboring in the work of the gospel, he labored very much, yea, sometimes night and day, in a handicraft trade to procure subsistence that he might not be chargeable to others, and so hinder the gospel of Christ: "For ye remember, brethren, our labor and travail, for laboring night and day, because we would not be chargeable unto any of you, we preached unto you the gospel of God" (1 Thess. 2:9). And he continued this course of labor as long as he lived. He never was weary in well-doing; and though he met with continual opposition and thousands of difficulties, yet nothing discouraged him. But he kept on pressing forward in this course of hard, constant labor to the end of his life, as appears by what he says just before his death: "I am now ready to be offered, and the time of my departure is at hand. I have fought a good fight, I have finished my course, I have kept the faith" (2 Tim. 4:6–7).

And the effects and fruits of the apostle's labors witnessed for him. The world was blessed by the good he did; not one nation only, but multitudes of nations. The effects of his labors were so great in so many nations before he had labored twenty years that the heathens called it his turning the world upside down (Acts 17:6). This very man was the chief instrument in the great work of God: the calling of the Gentiles and the conversion of the Roman world. And he seems to have done more good—far more good—than any other man ever did from the beginning of the world to this day. He lived after his conversion not much more than thirty years; and in those thirty years he did more than a thousand men commonly do in an age.

This example may well make us reflect upon ourselves and consider how little we do for Christ and for our fellow creatures. We profess to be Christians as well as the apostle Paul, and Christ is worthy that we should serve him as Paul did. But how small are our labors for God and Christ and our fellow creatures! Though many of us keep ourselves busy, how are our labor and strength spent, and with what is our time filled up? Let us consider ourselves a little, and the manner of our spending our time. We labor to provide for ourselves and families, to maintain ourselves in credit, and to make our part good among men. But is that all for which we are sent into the world? Did he who made us and gave us our powers of mind and strength of body, and who gives us our time and our talents, give them to us chiefly to be spent in this manner, or in serving him? Many years have rolled over the heads of some of us, and what have we lived for; what have we been doing all this time? How much is the world better for us? Were we here only to eat and to drink, and to devour the good which the earth produces? Many of the blessings of Providence have been conferred upon us, and where is the good that we have done in return? If we had never been born, or if we had died in infancy, of how much good would the world have been deprived?

Such reflections should be made with concern by those who pretend to be Christians. For certainly God does not plant vines in his vineyard except for the fruit which he expects they should bring forth. He does not hire laborers into his vineyard but to do service. They who live only for themselves live in vain, and shall at last be cut down as cumberers of the earth. Let the example of Paul make us more diligent to do good for the time to come. Men who do but little good are very ready to excuse themselves, and to say that God has not succeeded their endeavors. But is it any wonder that we have not been succeeded when we have been no more engaged? When God sees any person thoroughly and earnestly engaged, continuing in it, and really faithful, he is wont to succeed them in some good measure. You see how wonderfully he succeeded the great labors of the apostle.

EXERCISING GREAT SKILL

Third. He did not only encounter great labors, but he exercised also his utmost skill and contrivances for the glory of God and the good of his fellow creatures: "Being crafty, I caught you with guile" (2 Cor. 12:16). How do the men of the world not only willingly labor to obtain worldly good, but how much craft and subtlety do they use? And let us consider how it is here among ourselves. How many are our contrivances to secure and advance our own worldly concerns! Who can reckon up the number of all the schemes that have been formed among us to gain money and honors, and to accomplish particular worldly designs? How subtle are we to avoid those things that might hurt us in our worldly interest, and to baffle the designs of those who may be endeavoring to hurt us! But how little is contrived for the advancement of religion and the good of our neighbors! How many schemes are laid by men to promote their worldly designs where one is laid for the advancement of the kingdom of Christ and the good of men! How frequent are the meetings of neighbors to determine how they may best advance such and such worldly affairs! But how seldom are there such meetings to revive sinking religion, to maintain and advance the credit of the gospel, and to accomplish charitable designs for the advancement of Christ's kingdom and the comfort and well-being of mankind! May not these considerations justly be a source of lamentation? How many men are wise in promoting their worldly interests; but what a shame it is that so few show themselves wise as serpents and harmless as doves for Christ! And how commonly is it the reverse of what the apostle advises the Christian Romans: "I would have you be wise unto that which is good, and simple concerning evil" (Rom. 16:19). Is it not often on the contrary with professing Christians, as it was with the people of Judah and Jerusalem: "They are wise to do evil, but to do good they have no knowledge"?

FOREGOING THINGS LAWFUL

Fourth. The apostle Paul did willingly forego those things that were in themselves lawful for the furtherance of the interests of religion and the good of men. Thus, marriage was a thing lawful for the apostle Paul as well as for other men, as he himself asserts; but he did not use the liberty he had in this matter because he thought he might be under greater advantages to spread the gospel in a single than a married state. So it was lawful for the apostle to take the other course of life, as in eating and drinking and freely using all kinds of wholesome food. And it was in itself a thing lawful for the apostle to demand a maintenance of those to whom he preached. But he forbore those things because he supposed that, in his circumstances and in the circumstances of the church of Christ in that day, he could more advance the interests of religion and the good of men without them. For the gospel's sake and for the good of men, he was willing to forego all the outward advantages he could derive from them: "Wherefore if meat make my brother to offend, I will eat not meat while the world standeth, lest I make my brother to offend" (1 Cor. 8:13). He would not only avoid those things that were useless in themselves, but those also that gave any occasion to sin or which led or exposed either himself or others to sin. Then it follows in the next chapter:

> Am I not an apostle? Am I not free? Have I not seen Jesus Christ our Lord? Are not ye my work in the Lord? If I be not an apostle unto others, yet doubtless I am to you; for the seal of mine apostleship are ye in the Lord. Mine answer to them that do examine me is this, Have we not power to eat and to drink? Have we not power to lead a sister about, a wife, as well as the other apostles, and as the brethren of the Lord, and Cephas? Or I only and Barnabas, have not we power to forbear working? (1 Cor. 9:1-6)

The apostle did not only forbear some little things, but he put himself to great difficulties by forbearing those things that were in themselves lawful. It cost him a great deal of labor of body to maintain himself. But yet he willingly labored, working with his own hands; and as he says, though he was free of all men, yet he made himself the servant of all, that he might gain the more. Let this induce such persons to consider themselves whether they act altogether as become Christians, who look upon it as a sufficient excuse for all the liberties they take that the things in which they allow themselves are in themselves lawful, that they are nowhere forbidden; though they cannot deny but that, considered in their circumstances, they are of ill tendency and expose them to temptation, and really tend to wound the credit and interest of religion and to be a stumbling-block to others, or as the apostle expresses it, tend to cause others to offend. But they uphold themselves with this, that the things which they practice are not absolutely unlawful in themselves, and therefore they will not hearken to any counsels to avoid them. They think with themselves that it is unreasonable they should be tied up so strictly, that they may not take one and another liberty, and must be so stiff and precise above others. But why did not he say within himself: It is unreasonable that I should deny myself lawful meat and drink merely to comply with the consciences of a few weak persons who are unreasonable in their scruples? Why should I deny myself the comforts of marriage; why should I deny myself the maintenance which Christ himself has ordained for ministers, only to avoid the objection of unreasonable men? But the apostle was of another spirit. What he aimed at was by any means to promote the interest of religion and the good of the church. And he had rather to forego all the common comforts and enjoyments of life than that religion should suffer.

READINESS TO SUFFER

Fifth. The apostle willingly endured innumerable and extreme sufferings for the honor of Christ and the good of men. His sufferings were very great; and that not only once or twice, but he went through a long series of sufferings that continued from the time of his conversion for as long as his life lasted, so that his life was not only a life of extraordinary labor, but a life of extreme sufferings also. Labors and sufferings were mixed together and attended each other to the end of the race which he ran. He endured sufferings of all kinds, even those that cannot consist in the loss of temporal things. He tells us he had suffered the loss of all things, all his former enjoyments, which he had before his conversion (Phil. 3:8). And he suffered many kinds of positive afflictions:

> But in all things approving ourselves as the ministers of God, in much patience, in afflictions, in necessities, in distresses, in stripes, in imprisonments, in tumults, in labors, in watchings, in fastings; by pureness, by knowledge, by long-suffering, by kindness, by the Holy Ghost, by love unfeigned, by the word of truth, by the power of God, by the armor of righteousness on the right hand and on the left, by honor and dishonor, by evil report and good report: as deceivers, and yet true; as unknown, and yet well known; as dying, and behold we live; as chastened, and not killed; as sorrowful, yet always rejoicing; as poor, yet making many rich; as hav-

ing nothing, and yet possessing all things. (2 Cor. 6:4–10)

None of the apostles went through so great and such various afflictions as he:

> Are they ministers of Christ? I am more; in labors more abundant, in stripes above measure, in prisons more frequent, in deaths oft. Of the Jews five times received I forty stripes save one. Thrice was I beaten with rods, once was I stoned, thrice I suffered shipwreck, a night and a day I have been in the deep; in journeyings often, in perils of waters, in perils of robbers, in perils by mine own countrymen, in perils by the heathen, in perils in the city, in perils in the wilderness, in perils in the sea, in perils among false brethren; in weariness and painfulness, in watchings often, in hunger and thirst, in fastings often, in cold and nakedness. (2 Cor. 11:23–27)

His sufferings were so extreme that he did not go through a series of sufferings merely, but might be said, as it were, to go through a series of deaths. He did in effect endure the pains of death over and over again almost continually, and therefore he expresses himself as he does: "Persecuted, but not forsaken; cast down, but not destroyed; always bearing about in the body the dying of the Lord Jesus, that the life also of Jesus might be made manifest in our body. For we which live are always delivered unto death for Jesus' sake, that the life also of Jesus might be made manifest in our mortal flesh" (2 Cor. 4:9–11).

And: "As it is written, 'For thy sake we are killed all the day long; we are accounted as sheep for the slaughter' " (Rom. 8:36). And: "I protest by your rejoicing, which I have in Christ Jesus our Lord, I die daily" (1 Cor. 15:31). He was so pursued and pressed by troubles, sometimes outward and inward troubles together, that he had no rest: "For when we were come into Macedonia, our flesh had no rest, but we were troubled on every side: without were fightings, within were fears" (2 Cor. 7:5). Sometimes his sufferings were so extreme that his nature seemed just ready to faint under them: "For we would not, brethren, have you ignorant of our trouble, which came to us in Asia, that we were pressed out of measure above strength, insomuch that we despaired even of life" (2 Cor. 1:8). And at last the apostle was deprived of his life. He suffered a violent death at Rome under the hand of that cruel tyrant Nero, soon after he wrote the second epistle to Timothy.

These things he endured for Christ's sake, for the advancement of his kingdom; as he says, he was always delivered to death for Jesus' sake. And those he endured also from love to men and from an earnest desire of their good: "Therefore I endure all things for the elect's sake, that they may also obtain the salvation which is in Christ Jesus with eternal glory" (2 Tim. 2:10). He knew what afflictions awaited him beforehand, but he would not avoid his duty because of such afflictions. He was so resolute in seeking Christ's glory and the good of men that he would pursue these objects, notwithstanding what might befall him:

> And now, behold, I go bound in the spirit unto Jerusalem, not knowing the things that shall befall me there; save that the Holy Ghost witnesseth in every city, saying that bonds and afflictions abide me. But none of these things move me, neither count I my life dear unto myself, so that I might finish my course with joy, and the ministry, which I have received of the Lord Jesus, to testify the gospel of the grace of God. (Acts 20:22–24)

Yet he went through them cheerfully and willingly, and delighted to do God's will and to promote others' good, though it was at his great cost: "Who now rejoice in my sufferings for you, and fill up that which is behind of the afflictions of Christ in my flesh for his body's sake, which is the church" (Col. 1:24). And he was never weary. He did not, after he had suffered a long time, excuse himself, and say he thought he had done his part.

Now here appears Christianity in its proper colors. To be of such a spirit as this is to be of such a spirit as Christ so often requires of us, if we would be his disciples. This is to sell all and give to the poor. This is to take up the cross daily and follow Christ. To have such a spirit as this is to have good evidence of being a Christian indeed, a thorough Christian, one who has given himself to Christ without reserve; one who hates father and mother and wife and children and sisters, yea, and his own life also; one who

---

loses his life for Christ's sake, and so shall find it. And though it is not required of all that they should endure so great sufferings as Paul did, yet it is required and absolutely necessary that many Christians should be in a measure of this spirit, should be of a spirit to lose all things and suffer all things for Christ, rather than not obey his commands and seek his glory. How well may our having such an example as this set before our eyes make us ashamed, who are so backward now and then to lose little things, to put ourselves a little out of our way, to deny ourselves some convenience, to deny our sinful appetites, or to incur the displeasure of a neighbor. Alas! What thought have we of Christianity to make much of such things as these; to make so many objections, to keep back, and contrive ways to excuse ourselves, when a little difficulty arises! What kind of thoughts had we of being Christians when we first undertook to be such, or first pretended a willingness to be Christians? Did we never sit down and count the cost, or did we cast it up at this rate, that we thought the whole sum would not amount to such little sufferings as lie in our way?

STUDY QUESTIONS

1. Below are listed the five virtues toward God and men that Edwards discerned in Paul, and that he recommends for us. To the right of each, enter a word or phrase that describes the *opposite* of that virtue, as shown in the example provided:

THE VIRTUES OF PAUL	OPPOSITES
Public-spiritedness ———————	A strictly private person
Diligence in doing good	
Exercising great skill	
Foregoing things lawful	
Readiness to suffer	

2. Connect these opposites with a line, as in the example. Then, put a mark on the line indicating where you think most Christians whom you know would fall. For example, if they are more public-spirited than private, your "X" will be closer to the former than the latter. Do this for each of the pairs. Be prepared to explain why you marked them the way you did.

3. Summarize the state of the church today as you have experienced it. How are we doing when it comes to following Paul's example in these virtues? Where do you think we most need to improve? Can you suggest some ways in which we might begin to do that?

4. Review chapters 4–6 on the virtues of Paul. In which of these virtues do you most need to improve? What steps can you take to begin laying out a plan for improving in these virtues? Why do you think it would be good for you to do this?

5. Review the goals you set for this study at the end of chapter 1. Are you making progress? Do you need to revise or add to your goals in any way?

❋ *Chapter 7* ❋

FOLLOWING PAUL'S EXAMPLE

Edwards brings his discussion to a close, arguing that, since Paul was the greatest teacher of the Christian church, he should be our greatest example of the pursuit of holiness in the Lord. After a summary of his argument, Edwards offers seven considerations and four exhortations to encourage us to follow the example of this great apostle.

I now proceed to show under what special obligations we are to follow the good example of this apostle. Beside the obligation that rests upon us to follow the good example of all, and beside the eminence of his example, there are some special reasons why we are under greater obligations to be influenced by the good example of this great apostle than by the very same example in others. This appears if we consider [the following.]

PAUL'S CALLING AS A TEACHER OF THE CHURCH

Teachers as examples

In general, those whom God has especially appointed to be teachers in the Christian church he has also set to be examples in his church. It is part of the charge that belongs to teachers to be examples to others. It is one thing that belongs to their work and office. So this is part of the charge that the apostle gives to Timothy: "Be thou an example of the believers, in word, in conversation, in charity, in spirit, in faith, in purity" (1 Tim. 4:12). The same charge is given to Titus: "In all things showing thyself a pattern of good works" (Titus 2:7). And this is part of the charge the apostle Peter gives to the elders and teachers of the Christian church: "The elders which are among you, I exhort: feed the flock of God. . . . Neither being lords over God's heritage, but being examples to the flock" (1 Peter 5:1-3). Thus Christ, the chief Shepherd of the sheep, whom God ordained to be the greatest teacher, he also ordained to be the greatest example to his church. And so those shepherds and teachers that are under him, according as they are appointed to be teachers, are also to be examples.

They are to be guides of the flock in two ways, namely, by teaching and by example, as shepherds lead their flocks in two ways, partly by their voice by calling them, and partly by going before them and by leading the way. And indeed guiding by word and guiding by example are but two different ways of teaching; and therefore both alike belong to the office of teachers in the Christian church. But if this be so, if God has especially set those to be examples in the Christian church whom he has made its teachers, then it will follow that, wherever they have left us good examples, those examples are especially to be regarded. For God has doubtless made the duty of teachers toward the church and the duty of the church toward her teachers to answer to one another. And therefore the charge is mutual. The charge is not only to teachers to set good examples, but the charge is to the church to regard and follow their good examples: "Remember them which have the rule over you, which have spoken unto you the word of God, whose faith follow, considering the end of their conversation" (Heb. 13:7). It is with respect to the good examples of the teachers of the Christian church, as it is with their words, their instructions, and exhortations. We ought to hear good instructions and good counsels of anyone, let him be whom he may. But yet we are under special obligations to hearken to the good instructions and examples of those whom God has made our teachers; for that is the very office to which God has appointed them to teach and to counsel us.

Paul as teacher

There are two things that are to be observed in particular of the apostle Paul, which, from the foregoing general observation, will show that we are under very special obligations to regard and follow his good example.

First. God hath appointed the apostle Paul not only to be a greater teacher of the Christian church in that age in which he lived, but the principal teacher of his church of any mere man in all succeeding ages. He was set of God not only to teach the church then, when he lived, but God has made him our teacher by his inspired writings. The Christian church is taught by the apostle still, and has been in every age since he lived. It is not with the penmen of the Scriptures as it is with other teachers of the Christian church. Other teachers are made the teachers of a particular flock in the age in which they live. But the penmen of the Scriptures God hath made to be the teachers of the church universal in all ages. And therefore, as particular congregations ought to follow the good examples of their pastors, the church universal in all ages ought to observe and follow the good examples of the prophets and apostles who are penmen of the Scriptures, in all ages. So the apostle James commands us to take the ancient prophets for our example, because they have been appointed of God to be our teachers, and have spoken to us in the name of the Lord: "Take, my brethren, the prophets, who have spoken in the name of the Lord, for an example of suffering and affliction and patience" (James 5:10). The prophets and apostles, in that God has made them penmen of the Scriptures, are, next to Christ, the foundation of the church of God: "Built on the foundation of the prophets and apostles, Jesus Christ himself being the chief corner-stone" (Eph. 2:20). And Paul, above all the penmen of the Scriptures, is distinguished of God as being made by him the principal teacher of the Christian church of any mere man. Moses taught gospel truths under types and shadows, whereby he did, as it were, put a veil over his face. But Paul used great plainness of speech (2 Cor. 3:12–13). Moses was a minister of the Old Testament and of the letter that kills. But the apostle Paul is the principal minister of the

New Testament, of the spirit and not of the letter (2 Cor. 3:6). Christ has empowered this apostle to be the penmen of more of the New Testament than any other man, and it is by him chiefly that we have the great doctrines of it explained. And God has actually made this apostle the principal founder of the Christian church under Christ. He doubtless did more toward it than all the other apostles, and therefore is to be looked upon as the principal shepherd under Christ of the whole flock of Christ, which is a great obligation on the flock to regard and follow his good example.

Second. We, who are Gentiles, are especially under obligations to regard his teaching and example, because it has been mainly by means of this apostle that we have been brought into the Christian church. He was the great apostle of the Gentiles, the main instrument of that great work of God, the calling of the Gentiles. It was chiefly by his means that all the countries of Europe came by the gospel. And so it was through his hands that our nation came by the gospel. They either had the gospel from him immediately, or from those who had it from him. Had it not been for the labors of this apostle, our nation might have remained to this day in gross heathenism. This consideration should especially engage us to regard him as our guide, and should endear his good example to us. The apostle often exhorts those churches, as the church of Corinth, Philippi, and others which he had converted from heathenism, and to which he had been a spiritual father, to be followers of him wherein he followed Christ. And we are

some of them. We have been the more remarkably converted from heathenism by this apostle, and we ought to
acknowledge him as our spiritual father. And we are obliged
to follow his good example as children should follow the
good example of their parents.

APPLICATION

I now proceed to a general application of the whole that
has been said on this subject, which may be by way of
exhortation to all earnestly to endeavor to follow the good
example of this great apostle.

Summary

We have heard what a spirit the apostle manifested and
after what manner he lived in the world; how earnestly he
sought his own salvation, and that not only before, but also
after, his conversion; and how earnestly cautious he was to
avoid eternal damnation long after he had obtained a saving interest in Christ. We have heard how strong he was in
faith, how great was his love to his Lord and Savior, and
how he was not ashamed of the gospel, but gloried in the
cross of Christ; how he abounded in prayer and praise; how
he condemned the wealth and pleasures and glory of the
world; how contented he was with the allotments of Providence; how prudent and cautious he was in giving an
account of his achievements, lest he should represent more
of himself in words than men should see of him in deeds.

We have heard how much he suffered under abuses, how he loved his enemies, how he delighted in peace, and rejoiced with those who rejoiced and wept with those who wept, and delighted in the fellowship of God's people, and how courteous he was in his behavior toward others. We have heard of what a public spirit he was; how greatly concerned for the prosperity of Christ's kingdom and the good of his church; how diligent, laborious, and indefatigable in his endeavors to do good; how he studied for ways and means to promote this end; how he exercised his skill and contrivance, willingly foregoing those things that were in themselves lawful, and willingly enduring innumerable and extraordinary sufferings. My exhortation now is to imitate this example; and to enforce this, I desire that several things may be considered.

That we have so much written of Paul

Let it be considered why it is that we have so much written of the good example of this apostle, unless that we might follow it. We often read those things in the Holy Scriptures which have now been set before us on this subject; and to what purpose, unless we apply them to ourselves? We had as good never have been informed how well the apostle behaved himself, if we do not endeavor to follow him. We all profess to be Christians, and we ought to form our notions of Christianity from what is written in the Scriptures by the prophets, and from the precepts and excellent examples that are there set before us. One reason why many professors live no better, walk no more amiably, and are in so many things so unlovely is that they have not good notions of Christianity. They do not seem to have a right idea of that religion that is taught us in the New Testament. They have not well learned Christ. The notions that some persons entertain of Christianity are very distorted and ill conformed to the gospel. The notions of others are very erroneous. They lay the chief stress wrong, upon things on which it ought not to be laid. They place religion almost altogether in some particular duties, leaving out others of great weight, and, it may be, the weightier matters of the law. And the reason why they have no better notions of Christianity is because they take their notions of it chiefly from those sources whence they ought not to take them. Some take them from the general cry or voice of the people among whom they live. They see that others place religion merely, if not almost wholly, in such and such things. And hence their notions of Christianity are formed. Or they take their notions from the example of particular individuals now living who are in great reputation for godliness. And their notion of Christianity is that it consists of being like such persons. Hence they never have just notions of religion: "They, measuring themselves by themselves, and comparing themselves among themselves, are not wise" (2 Cor. 10:12).

If we would have right notions of Christianity, we should observe those in whom it shone, of whom we have an account in the Scriptures. For they are the examples that God himself has selected to set before us to that end, that from thence we might form our notions of religion; and especially the example of the apostle. God knows how to select examples. If therefore we would have right notions of Christianity, we ought to follow the good example of the apostle Paul. He was certainly a Christian indeed, and an eminent Christian. We have God's abundant testimony. But Christianity is in itself an amiable thing, and so it appeared in the example of this apostle. And if the professors of it would form their notions of it from such examples as those, rather than from any particular customs and examples that we have now, it would doubtless appear much more amiable in their practice than it now does; it would win others. They would not be a stumbling-block. Their light would shine. They would command reverence and esteem, and be of powerful influence.

That Paul shows us the way to a happy life

If we follow the good example which this apostle has set us, it will secure to us the like comfortable and sweet influence of God that he enjoyed through the course of his life. Let us consider what a happy life the apostle lived, what peace of conscience and joy in the Holy Ghost he possessed: "For our rejoicing is this, the testimony of our conscience" (2 Cor. 1:12). How did he abound with comfort and joy, even in the midst of the greatest afflictions: "Blessed be God, even the Father of our Lord Jesus Christ, the Father of mercies, and the God of all comfort. Who comforteth us in all our tribulation, that we may be able to comfort them which are in any trouble, by the comforts wherewith we ourselves are comforted of God. For as the sufferings of Christ abound in us, so our consolation also aboundeth in Christ" (2 Cor. 1:3–5). In all his tribulation his joy was exceedingly great. He seems to want words to express the greatness of the joy which he possessed continually. He says he was filled with comfort, and was exceedingly joyful: "I am filled with comfort, I am exceeding joyful in all our tribulation" (2 Cor. 7:4). How does the apostle's love seem to overflow with joy! "As sorrowful, yet always rejoicing; as poor, yet making many rich; as having nothing, yet possessing all things. O ye Corinthians, our mouth is open unto you, our heart is enlarged" (2 Cor. 6:10–11). How happy is such a life! How well is such happiness worth pursuing! We are ourselves the occasion of our own wounds and troubles. We bring darkness on our own souls. Professing Christians, by indulging their sloth, seek their own ease and comfort; but they defeat their own aim. The most laborious and the most self-denying Christians are the most happy. There are many who are complaining of their darkness and inquiring what they shall do for light and the comfortable presence of God.

That this is the way through temptation

This would be the way to be helped against temptation and to triumph over our spiritual enemies as the apostle did. Satan assaulted him violently, and men continually persecuted him. The powers of hell combined against him. But God was with him and made him more than a conqueror. He lived a life of triumph: "Now thanks be unto God, who always causeth us to triumph in Christ" (2 Cor. 2:14). Let us consider what an excellent privilege it would be thus to be helped against temptation. What a grief of mind is it to be so often overcome.

That Paul shows us the way to intimacy with God

This would secure us honor from God and an extraordinary intimacy with him. Moses enjoyed a great intimacy with God, but the apostle Paul in some respects a greater. Moses conversed with God in Mount Sinai. Paul was caught up to the third heavens. He had abundant visions and revelations more than he has told us, lest any should think him to boast. He was favored with more of the miraculous gifts of the Holy Spirit than any other person. And though we cannot expect to be honored with intimacy with heaven in just the same way, yet if we in good earnest apply ourselves, we may have greater and greater intimacy, so that we may come with boldness and converse with God as a friend.

That this way we become blessings to others

This would be the way to make us great blessings in the world. The apostle, by means of such a spirit and such a behavior as you have heard, was made the greatest blessing to the world of any who ever lived on earth, except the man Christ Jesus himself. Wherever he went, there went a blessing with him. To have him enter a city was commonly made a greater mercy to it than if the greatest monarch on earth had come there scattering his treasures around him among the inhabitants. Wherever he went, there did, as it were, a light shine about him, seemingly to enlighten the benighted children of men. Silver and gold had he none. But what he imparted to many thousands was worth more to them than if he had bestowed upon them the richest jewels of which the Roman emperor was possessed. And he was not only a blessing to that generation, but has been so since his death, by the fruits of what he did in his lifetime, the foundations he then laid, and by the writings which he has left for the good of mankind, to the end of the world. He then was, and ever since has been, a light to the church next in brightness to the Sun of righteousness. And it was by means of his excellent spirit and excellent behavior that he became such a blessing. Those were the things that God made useful in him for doing so much good. And if we should imitate the apostle in such a spirit and behavior, the undoubted consequence would be that we also should be made great blessings in the world; we should not live in vain, but should carry a blessing with us wherever we went. Instead of being cumberers of the ground, multitudes would be fed with our fruit and would have reason to praise and bless God that he ever gave us a being. Now, how melancholy a consideration may it be to any persons who have lived to no purpose that the world would have been deprived of nothing if they had never been born; and it may be, have been better without them than with them! How desirable it is to be a blessing! How great was the promise made to Abraham: "In thee shall all the families of the earth be blessed" (Gen. 12:3)!

That such a life is good preparation for dying

For us to follow the good example of the apostle Paul would be the way for us to die as he did: "For I am now ready to be offered, and the time of my departure is at hand. I have fought a good fight, I have finished my course, I have kept the faith; henceforth there is laid up for me a crown of righteousness, which the Lord, the righteous Judge, shall give me at that day" (2 Tim. 4:6–8).

That such a life would secure a crown of glory

This would secure us a distinguished crown of glory hereafter. It is thought by some, and not without great probability, that the apostle Paul is the very next in glory to the man Jesus Christ himself. This is probably from his having done more good than any, and from his having done it through so great labors and sufferings. The apostle tells us, "Every man shall receive his own reward according to his labor" (1 Cor. 3:8).

CONCLUDING ENCOURAGEMENTS

I shall conclude with mentioning some things as encouragements for us to endeavor to follow the excellent example of the great apostle. Many may be ready to say that it is vain for them to try. The apostle was a person so greatly distinguished; it is vain for them to endeavor to be like him. But for your encouragement, consider:

1. That the apostle was a man of like passions with us. He had naturally the same heart, the same corruptions; was under the same circumstances, the same guilt, and the same condemnation. There is this circumstance that attends the apostle's example to encourage us to endeavor to imitate

him which did not attend the example of Christ. And yet we are called upon to imitate the example of Christ. This is probably one main reason why not only the example of Christ, but also those of mere men are set before us in the Scriptures. Though you may think you have not great reason to hope to come up to the apostle's degree, yet that is no reason why you should not make his good example your pattern, and labor, as far as in you lies, to copy after him.

2. This apostle, before he was converted, was a very wicked man and a vile persecutor. He often speaks of it himself. He sinned against great light.

3. He had much greater hindrances and impediments to eminent holiness from without than any of us have. His circumstances made it more difficult for him.

4. The same God, the same Savior, and the same head of divine influence are ready to help our sincere endeavors, that helped him. Let us therefore not excuse ourselves, but in good earnest endeavor to follow so excellent an example. And then, however weak we are in ourselves, we may hope to experience Christ's support and be able to say from our own experience, as the apostle did before him, "When I am weak, then am I strong" (2 Cor. 12:10).

STUDY QUESTIONS

1. Summarize Edwards's argument for following Paul's example because he was the most eminent teacher of the

church. Why should this encourage us to take up the pursuit of holiness in the Lord after the example of Paul?

2. Where do some people look for guidance in living the Christian life? Review Edwards's comments on this point. Is this still valid today? Why is this not a sufficient place to gather our "notions" about what the Christian life should be like? Why is Paul's example a better place to look?

3. How can following Paul's example help us to draw closer to the Lord, to become more dependent on him, to have a greater sense of his daily presence with us, and to help us focus on those "unseen things" which are so important to a vibrant faith (Heb. 11:1)?

4. Is it important to you to be a blessing to others? Which aspects of Paul's example, summarized at the beginning of the application section of this chapter, would you most like to see more of in your own life? How would that help you to be more of a blessing to the people around you?

5. Paul provides an excellent example for us of what it means to *pursue* holiness in the Lord, as well as to what becoming holy *looks like*. What is the most important thing you have learned from chapters 1–7 about pursuing holiness in the Lord after the example of the apostle Paul? How will you put that into practice in your life?

❈ *Part 2* ❈

Hope and Comfort Usually Follow Genuine Humiliation and Repentance

❊ *Chapter 8* ❊

HOPE AND COMFORT
AT CONVERSION

As we saw in our last chapter, the life of holiness is the life of happiness—of hope and comfort in the Lord. This is a state much to be desired and heartily pursued. But the pursuit of holiness can be a daunting and frustrating endeavor. One reason why this is so is that we discover in our journey of sanctification so much for which we need to repent, and so much which brings us trouble and humiliation. But God uses these experiences to advance us in our calling and bring us hope and comfort. Edwards shows us that this is so, even from our first coming to faith in Jesus Christ. Leaving nothing to chance, and assuming nothing of his hearers, Edwards insists that the life of happiness, hope, and comfort we seek—the life of holiness—will never be ours apart from an initial conversion to Christ and the hating of all sin.

HOSEA 2:15
And I will give her vineyards from thence, and the valley of Achor for a door of hope: and she shall sing there, as in the days of her youth, and as in the day when she came up out of the land of Egypt.

INTRODUCTION

In the context, the church of Israel is first threatened with the awful desolation which God was about to bring upon her for her dealing so falsely and treacherously with God; because though, in the bold language of the prophet, she had been married to God, she had yet gone after other lovers and had committed adultery with them. "For she said, I will go after my lovers, that give me my bread, and my water, my wool and my flax, mine oil and my drink" (Hos. 2:5). Therefore God threatened that he would strip her naked and set her as in the day that she was born, and make her as a wilderness, and set her like a dry land, and slay her with thirst, and that he would discover her lewdness in the sight of her lovers, and destroy her vines and fig trees, and make them a forest. So the prophet goes on terribly threatening her to the end of the thirteenth verse. And those things were fulfilled in the captivity of Israel in the land of Assyria.

But in the verse preceding the text, and in the remainder of the chapter, there follows a gracious promise of mercy, which God would show her in the days of the gospel. "Therefore, behold, I will allure her, and bring her into the wilderness, and speak comfortably unto her. And I will give her her vineyards from thence, and the valley of Achor for a door of hope: and she shall sing there, as in the days of her youth, and as in the day when she came up out of the land of Egypt." "I will allure her," that is, I will court or woo her again, as a young man woos a virgin whom he desires to make his wife. God, for her committing adultery with other lovers, had threatened that he would give her a bill of divorce, as in verse 2: "Plead with your mother, plead; for she is not my wife, neither am I her husband." But here in the latter part of the chapter, God promises that in the gospel times he would make her his wife again, as in the sixteenth verse: "And it shall be at that day that thou shalt call me Ishi;" that is, "my husband." And so in verses 19 and 20: "And I will betroth thee unto me forever; yea, I will betroth thee unto me forever in righteousness, and in judgment, in lovingkindness, and in mercies; I will even betroth thee unto me in faithfulness." Here, in the fourteenth verse, God promises that he will woo her, and in the latter part of the verse, he shows in what manner he will deal with her when he is about to woo or allure her. He would first bring her into the wilderness; that is, he would bring her into trouble and distress, and so humble her, and then allure her by speaking comfortably or pleasantly to her, as a young man does to a maid whom he woos. Then follow the words of the text.

God gives his people hope and comfort

We may observe what God would give to the children of Israel, namely, hope and comfort. He promises to give her vineyards, which, being spiritually interpreted as most of the prophecies of gospel times are to be interpreted, signifies spiritual comforts. Vineyards afford wine, which is comfort to those who are of heavy hearts: "Give wine to those that are of heavy hearts" (Prov. 31:6). Wine is to make glad the heart of man (Ps. 104:15). Gospel rest and peace are sometimes prophesied of, under the metaphor of every man's sitting under his vine and under his own fig tree. God promises to give her hope, to open a door of hope for her, and to give her songs; that is, to give her spiritual joy, and both cause and disposition joyfully to sing praises to God.

How God would bestow these benefits

We observe after what manner God would bestow those benefits.

First, they should be given after great trouble and abasement. Before she had this hope and comfort given, she should be brought into great trouble and distress to humble her. He promises to give her her vineyards from thence; that is, from the wilderness spoken of in the foregoing verse, into which it is said that God would bring her, before he spoke comfortably to her. God would bring her into the wilderness, and then give her vineyards. God's bringing her into the wilderness was to humble her and fit her to receive vineyards, and to make her see her dependence on God for them, that she might not attribute her enjoyment of them to her idols, as she had done before, for which reason God took them away, as in the twelfth verse: "And I will destroy her vines and her fig trees, whereof she hath said, 'These are my rewards that my lovers have given me; and I will make them a forest.' " There it is threatened that God will turn her vineyards into a forest, or wilderness. Here is it promised that he would turn the wilderness into vineyards, as in Isaiah 32:15: "Until the Spirit be poured on us from on high, and the wilderness be a fruitful field, and the fruitful land be counted for a forest." She should first be in a wilderness, where she shall see that she cannot help herself, nor any of her idols help, or give her any vineyards. And then God will help her, that she shall see that it is God, and not any of her idols or lovers. God would first bring her into a wilderness, and thence give her vineyards, as God first brought the children of Israel into a dreadful wilderness. So God opened a door of hope to them in the valley of Achor, which is a word that signifies trouble, and was so called from the trouble which the children of Israel suffered by the sin of Achor.

So God is wont first to make their sin a great trouble to them, an occasion of a great deal of distress, before he opens a door of hope. God promises to make her sing there as in the days of her youth, and as in the day when she came up out of the land of Egypt. This plainly refers to the joyful song which Moses and the children of Israel sang when they came up out of the Red Sea. The children of Israel there had great joy and comfort; but just before they had great trouble. They had been in extreme distress by the oppression of their taskmasters; and just before this triumphant song, they were brought to extremity and almost to despair, when Pharaoh and the Egyptians appeared ready to swallow them up.

Second, this hope and comfort should be bestowed on the slaying and forsaking of sin. That is the trouble of the soul. It should be given in the valley of Achor, which was the valley where the troubler of Israel was slain, as you may see in Joshua 7:26; and the place where the children of Israel sang, when they came up out of the land of Egypt. The eastern shore of the Red Sea was the place where they saw their enemies and old taskmasters, the types of men's lusts, which are sinners' taskmasters, lie dead on the sea shore, and of whom they took their final leave. And God had told them that their enemies, whom they had seen that day, they should see no more forever.

Doctrine. God is wont to cause hope and comfort to arise in the soul after trouble and humbling for sin, and according as the troubler is slain and forsaken. I would show:

I. That it is thus with respect to the first true hope and comfort which is given to the soul at conversion.

II. That God is wont to bestow hope and comfort on Christians from time to time in this way.

It is God's manner to bestow hope and comfort on a soul in conversion after trouble and humbling for sin. Under this head are three things to be observed: (1) the trouble itself; (2) the cause, namely, sin; (3) the humbling.

THE TROUBLE ITSELF

Trouble in spite of ease

Souls are wont to be brought into trouble before God bestows true hope and comfort. The corrupt hearts of men naturally incline to stupidity and senselessness before God comes with the awakening influences of his Spirit. They are quiet and secure; they have not true comfort and hope, and yet they are quiet; they are at ease. They are in miserable slavery, and yet seek not a remedy. They say, as the children of Israel did in Egypt to Moses, "Let us alone, that we may serve the Egyptians." But if God has a design of mercy to them, it is his manner, before he bestows true hope and comfort on them, to bring them into trouble, to distress them, and spoil their ease and false quietness, and to rouse them out of their old resting and sleeping places, and to bring them into a wilderness. They are brought into trouble, and sometimes into exceedingly great trouble and distress, so that they can take no comfort in those things in which they used to take comfort. Their hearts are pinched and stung, and they can find no ease in anything. They have, as it were, an arrow sticking fast in them, which causes grievous and continual pain, an arrow which they cannot shake off or pull out. The pain and anguish of it drinks up their spirit. Their worldly enjoyments were a sufficient good before, but they are not now. They wander about with wounded hearts, seeking rest and finding none, like one wandering in a dry and parched wilderness under the burning, scorching heat of the sun, seeking for some shadow where he may sit down and rest, but finding none. Wherever he goes the beams of the sun scorch him; or he seeks some fountain of cool water to quench his thirst, but finds not a drop. He is like David in his trouble, who wandered about in the wilderness, Saul pursuing him wherever he went, driving and hunting him from one wilderness to another, from one mountain to another, and from one cave to another, giving him no rest.

Trouble the plight of sinners

To such sinners, all things look dark, and they know not what to do or whither to turn. If they look forward or backward, to the right hand or the left, all is gloom and perplexity. If they look to heaven, behold darkness; if they look to earth, behold trouble and darkness and dimness of anguish. Sometimes they hope for relief, but they are disappointed, and so again and again they travail in pain, and a dreadful sound is in their ears. They are terrified and affrighted, and they seek refuge as a poor creature pursued by an enemy. He flies to one refuge and there is beset, and that fails; then he flies to another, and then is driven out of that. And his enemies grow thicker and thicker about, encompassing him on every side. They are like those of whom we read in Isaiah 24:17–18. Fear and the pit and the snare are upon them, and when they flee from the noise of the fear they are taken in the pit; and if they come up out of the pit, they are taken in the snare, so that they know not what to do. They are like the children of Israel while Achor troubled them. They go forth against their enemies, and they are smitten down and flee before them. They call on God, but he does not answer nor seem to regard them. Sometimes they find something in which they take pleasure for a little time, but it soon vanishes away and leaves them in greater distress than before. And sometimes they are brought to the very borders of despair. Thus they are brought into the wilderness, and into the valley of Achor, or of trouble.

The Cause — Sin

The disease of the soul

Sin is the trouble or the cause of this trouble. Sin is the disease of the soul, and such a disease as will, if the soul is not benumbed, cause exceeding pain. Sin brings guilt, and that brings condemnation and wrath. All this trouble arises from conviction of sin. Awakened sinners are convinced that they are sinful. Before, the sinner thought well of himself, or was not convinced that he was very sinful. But now he is led to reflect first on what he has done, how wickedly he has spent his time, what wicked acts or practices he has been guilty of. And afterwards, in the progress of his awakenings, he is made sensible of something of the sin and plague of his heart. They are made sensible of the guilt and wrath which sin brings. The threatenings of God's law are set home, and they are made sensible that God is angry, and that his wrath is dreadful. They are led to consider of the dreadfulness of that punishment which God has threatened.

The role of fear in trouble

The affection or principle which is wrought upon to cause this trouble is fear. They are afraid of the punishment of sin, and God's wrath for it. They are commonly afraid of many things here in this world as the fruit of sin. They are afraid God will not hear their prayers, that he is so angry with them that he will never give them converting grace. They are afraid oftentimes that they have committed the unpardonable sin, or at least that they have been guilty of such sin as God will never pardon; that their day is past, and that God has given them up to judicial hardness of heart and blindness of mind. Or if they are not already, they are afraid they shall be. They are afraid oftentimes that the Spirit of God is not striving with them now, that their fears are from some other cause. Sometimes they are afraid that it is only the devil who terrifies and afflicts them, and that if the Spirit of God is striving with them, he will be taken from them, and they shall be left in a Christless state. They are afraid that if they seek salvation, it will be to no purpose, and that they shall only make their case worse and worse; that they are farther and farther from anything which is good, and that there is less probability now of their being converted than when they began to seek. Sometimes they fear that they have but a short time to live and that God will soon cast them to hell; that none ever were as they are, who ever found mercy; that their case is peculiar, and that all wherein they differ from others is for the worse. They have fears on every side. Oftentimes they are afraid of everything. Everything looks dark, and they are afraid that everything will prove ruinous to them.

But in the issue of all they are afraid they shall perish forever. They are afraid that when they die they shall go down to hell, and there have their portion appointed to them in everlasting burnings. This is the sum of all their fears. And the cause of this fear is a consciousness of the guilt of sin. It is sin which is the cruel taskmaster, which oppresses them and chastises them; and sin is the cruel

Pharaoh which pursues them. As the children of Israel, before they came to sing with joy after they came out of the land of Egypt, were under great trouble from their taskmasters, and sighed by reason of the hard bondage, and then were pursued, and put into dreadful fear at the Red Sea. It was their taskmasters who made them all this trouble. So it is sin which makes all the trouble which a sinner suffers under awakenings. Their trouble for sin is no gracious, godly sorrow for sin; for that does not arise merely from fear, but from love. It is not an evangelical, but legal repentance of which we are speaking, which is not from love of God, but only self-love.

THE HUMBLING

The end of trouble

The end of this trouble in those to whom God designs mercy is to humble them. God leads them into the wilderness before he speaks comfortably to them, for the same cause that he led the children of Israel into the wilderness before he brought them into Canaan, which, we are told, was to humble them: "And thou shalt remember all the way, which the Lord thy God led thee these forty years in the wilderness, to humble thee, and to prove thee, and to know what was in thine heart" (Deut. 8:2). Man naturally trusts in himself, and magnifies himself. And for man to enjoy only ease and prosperity and quietness tends to nourish and establish such a disposition: "Jeshurun waxed fat, and kicked" (Deut. 32:15). But by trouble and distress, and by a sense of the heavy load of guilt, God brings men down into the dust. God brings souls thus into the wilderness to show them their own helplessness; to let them see that they have nothing to which they can turn for help; to make them sensible that they are not rich and increased with goods, but wretched, miserable, poor, blind, and naked; to show them that they are utterly undone and ruined; to make them sensible of their exceeding wickedness; and to bring them to be sensible how justly God might cast them off forever.

Those legal troubles tend to show them their utter inability to help themselves, as their fears put them on using their utmost endeavors, and trying their utmost strength; and by continuing in that way their experience teaches them their weakness, and they find they can do nothing. It puts them upon repeated trials, and they have as repeated disappointments. But repeated disappointments tend to bring a man to give up the case, and to despair of help in that way in which he has tried for it. It tends to make men sensible of the utter insufficiency of their wisdom, and bring them to see their own exceeding blindness and ignorance. For fear and concern and distress necessarily put a person on intensely thinking and studying and contriving for relief. But when men have been thus trying their own wisdom and invention to their utmost, and find it fails, and signifies nothing, and is altogether to no purpose, it makes them more and more sensible of their weakness and blindness, and brings them to confess themselves fools, and blind as to those things which concern their relief. They are like one who is placed in the midst of a vast, hideous wilderness. At first it may be he may not be sensible but that he knows the way home, and can directly go in the way which leads out of the wilderness. But after he has tried and traveled awhile, and finds that he cannot find the way, and that he spends himself in vain, and only goes round and round, and comes to the same place again at last, he is brought to confess that he knows not where to go nor what to do, and that he is sensible that he is like one who is perfectly lost and altogether in darkness, and is brought at last to yield the case and stand still, and do nothing but call for help, that if possible anyone may hear and lead him in the wilderness.

Trouble leads to reflection on sin

For this end God leads men into the wilderness before he speaks comfortably to them. The troubles which they have for sin tend to bring them to be sensible how justly God may cast them off forever; and this brings them to reflect on their sins, for these are the things of which they are afraid. When a man is terribly afraid of things with which he is surrounded, this engages his eyes to behold; he looks intensely on them, and sees more and more how frightful and terrible they are. When they are in fear, they take much more notice of their sins than at other times. They think more how wickedly they have lived, and observe more the corrupt and wicked working of their own hearts, and so are more and more sensible what vile creatures they are. This makes them more and more sensible how angry

God is, and how terrible his anger is. They try to appease and to reconcile God by their own righteousness, but it fails. God still appears as an angry God, refusing to hear their prayers or appear for their help till they despair in their own righteousness and yield the case; and by more and more of a sight of themselves are brought to confess that they lie justly exposed to damnation, and have nothing by which to defend themselves. God appears more and more as a terrible being to them, till they have done with imaginations that they have anything sufficient to recommend them or reconcile them to such a God. Thus God is wont to bring the soul into trouble by reason of sin, and so to humble the soul, before he gives true hope and comfort in conversion.

THE SLAYING OF THE TROUBLER

No true hope without it

This hope and comfort are given upon the slaying of the troubler. Whatever troubles there are for sin, yet if the troubler is not slain, it cannot be expected but that there will be trouble still. Before there will be no true comfort. The soul may return to stupidity and carelessness, and may receive a false peace and hope, and sin be kept alive; but no true hope. Persons may be exceedingly troubled for sin, and yet sin be saved alive. Persons may seem to lament that they have done thus and thus, and weep many tears, and cry out of the sinfulness and wickedness, and yet the life of sin be whole in them. But if so, they never shall receive true comfort. They may refrain from sin; there may be a great reformation and exact life for a time, or there may be a total reformation of some particular ways of sin, and yet no true hope; because sin is only restrained; it is not slain. Many men are brought to restrain sin, and to give it slight wounds, who cannot be brought to kill it. Wicked men are loathe to kill sin. They have been very good friends to it ever since they have been in the world, and have always treated it as one of their most familiar and best friends. They have allowed it the best room in their hearts, and have given it the best entertainment they could, and they are very loathe to destroy it. But until this be done, God never will give them true comfort. If ever men come to have a true hope, they must do as the children of Israel did by Achan:

> And Joshua, and all Israel with him, took Achan, the son of Zerah, and the silver and the garment, and the wedge of gold, and his sons and his daughters, and his oxen, and his asses, and his sheep, and his tent, and all that he had; and they brought them unto the valley of Achor. And Joshua said, "Why hast thou troubled us? The Lord shall trouble thee this day." And all Israel stoned them with stones, and burned them with fire after they had stoned them with stones. And they raised over him a great heap of stones unto this day. So the Lord turned from the fierceness of his anger. Wherefore the name of that place was called the valley of Achor unto this day. (Josh. 7:24–26)

So if ever men come to have any true hope, they must take sin, which is the troubler, and all which belongs to it, even that which seems most dear and precious, though it be as choice as Achan's silver and wedge of gold, and utterly destroy them, and burn them with fire, to be sure to make a thorough end of them, as it were, bury them and raise over them a great heap of stones, to lay a great weight upon them, to make sure of it that they shall never rise more. Yea, and thus they must serve all his sons and daughters. They must not save some of the accursed brood alive. All the fruits of sin must be forsaken. There must not be some particular lust, some dear sinful enjoyment, some pleasant child of sin, spared: but all must be stoned and burned. If we do thus, we may expect to have trouble cease, and light to arise, as it was in the camp of Israel after the slaying of the troubler.

PRACTICE

Inquiry. Here it may be inquired, What is implied in slaying sin at conversion? And it implies these several things:

Conviction of evil

There must be a conviction of the evil of it as against God. All is carried on by conviction. Those legal troubles, which are before conversion, arise from some conviction of the being of sin and the guilt and danger of it. And the slaying of sin is by conviction of its evil and hateful nature. To slay the troubler, we must find him out, as the children of Israel did before they slew Achan. They rose early in the morning, and searched, and brought all Israel by their tribes; and then searched the tribe, which was taken by families, and the family by particular persons, and so found him.

To hate sin

It is to have the heart turned from, and turned against it, in hatred. The troubler is never slain but by a thorough and saving change of heart and renovation of nature, so that that which before loved sin and chose it, may now hate and abhor it, and may disrelish it and all its ways, and especially hate their former ways of sin.

To forsake and renounce it

Forsaking and renouncing it. Let men pretend what they may, their hearts are not turned from sin if they do not forsake it. He is not converted who is not really come to a disposition utterly to forsake all ways of sin. If ever sinners have true hope and comfort, they must take a final leave of sin, as the children of Israel did of the Egyptians at the Red Sea. Persons may have a great deal of trouble from sin, and many conflicts and struggles with it, and seem to forsake it for a time, and yet not forsake it finally; as the children of Israel had with the Egyptians. They had a long struggle with them before they were freed from them. How many judgments did God bring upon the Egyptians, before they would let them go? And sometimes Pharaoh seemed as if he would let them go; but yet when it came to the proof he refused. And when they departed from Rameses, doubtless they thought then they had got rid of them. They did not expect to see them anymore. But when they arrived at the Red Sea, and looked behind them, they saw them pursuing them. They found it a difficult thing wholly to get rid of them. But when they were drowned in the Red Sea, then they took an everlasting leave of them. The king and all the chiefs of them were dead; and therefore God said to them, "The Egyptians whom ye have seen today, ye shall see them again no more forever" (Ex. 14:13).

So sinners must not only part with sin for a little time, but they must forsake it forever, and be willing never to see or have anything to do with their old sinful ways and enjoyments. They must forsake that which is their iniquity, the sin which most easily besets them, and to which by their constitution or custom they have been most addicted; which has been, as it were, the dearest of all, and most respected, as a king among the army of sins; though that must be slain too, as Pharaoh, the king of the Egyptians, was in the Red Sea. And we must not do as Saul did, when God sent him to kill the Amalekites; but he saved the king of the Amalekites alive, which cost him his kingdom.

Embracing and trusting Christ

It implies embracing Christ, and trusting in him as the Savior from sin. We must look to him not only as a Savior from the punishment of sin, but we must receive and embrace him as a Savior from sin itself. We cannot deliver ourselves from sin. We cannot slay this enemy ourselves. He is too strong an enemy for us. We can no more slay sin ourselves than the children of Israel, who were themselves a poor feeble company, a mixed multitude, unprepared to resist such a force, could themselves slay Pharaoh, and all his mighty army with chariots and horsemen. It was Christ in the pillar of cloud and fire who fought for them. They had nothing to do but trust in him: "The Lord shall fight for you, and ye shall hold your peace" (Ex. 14:14). They could never have drowned the Egyptians in the sea. It was Christ who did it; for the pillar of cloud stood between them and the Israelites, and when they were up out of the sea, then Christ brought on them the waters of the sea. Our enemies must be drowned in the all-sufficient fountain and, as it were, sea of Christ's blood, as the Egyptians were in the Red Sea, and then we may sing, as the children of Israel did in the day when they came up out of the land of Egypt.

When sin is thus slain, then God is wont to open a door of hope, a door through which there flashes a sweet light out of heaven upon the soul. Then comfort arises, and then there is a new song in the mouth, even praise unto God.

STUDY QUESTIONS

1. Edwards leaves no stone unturned in his instruction about the life of happiness, hope, and comfort—the life of holiness. This life begins in the recognition of our sinfulness and need of a Savior, even Jesus. Review Edwards's discus-

sion of how Israel credited her well-being to idols—created things. Do people do this yet today? Have you ever done this? To what does this lead?

2. Does your own experience in coming to Christ mirror Edwards's description of being lost in a wilderness, desperate to find a way out? Explain.

3. Edwards emphasizes the fear of God in this chapter. We don't hear much about that today. Why do you suppose this is so? Do you think this is a subject we need to speak about more frequently in the church? What about in our work of evangelism? Why do you feel this way?

4. Review Edwards's discussion of what it means to "slay the troubler." Can you say that you have truly "slain" sin in your life, as Edwards describes? Or are you just involved in a bit of "reformation," or other attempt simply to set sin aside for a season? How do you typically try to deal with the sin you become aware of in your life?

5. Review the goals you set for this study at the end of chapter 1. How are you doing? Can you see any progress toward those goals?

❖ *Chapter 9* ❖

Hope and Comfort
for the Christian

The attainment of hope and comfort is the great reward of pursuing holiness in the Lord. But Christians often stumble along the way, falling into sin and a dark night of the soul. God allows them to linger awhile in darkness before he lifts them out into the newness of light and life once again. In this section of the sermon, Edwards guides us back onto the path when we, too, may occasionally lapse into grievous sin.

God is wont to bestow hope and comfort from time to time in the same manner on Christians. In the consideration of this matter I would show,

1. That Christians are frequently in darkness, and their hope is often greatly obscured.

2. That it is sin which is the occasion of this darkness.

3. Their darkness is not perpetual, but God is wont to cause hope and comfort to rise again.

4. Their trouble is commonly much increased a little before the renewal of light and hope.

5. That hope and comfort are renewed to them on the slaying of the troubler.

CHRISTIANS FREQUENTLY
IN DARKNESS

God's grace exempts some Christians from darkness

It is often the case that Christians are under darkness, and their hope is greatly clouded. God is wont to give his saints hope and comfort at their first conversion, which sometimes remains without any great interruption for a considerable time. And some Christians live abundantly more in the light than others. Some for many years together have but little darkness. God is pleased to distinguish them from their neighbors. He mercifully keeps them from those occasions of darkness into which he suffers others to fall, and gives them of the light of his countenance. God exercises his sovereignty in this matter, as he does in giving converting grace: as he bestows that on whom he pleases, so he bestows on some of those who are converted more light, on others less, according as it pleases him.

Types of darkness experienced by many

But many Christians meet with a great deal of darkness, and see times in which their hopes are much clouded. Sometimes the sweet and comfortable influences of God's Spirit are withdrawn. They were wont to have spiritual discoveries made of God and Christ to their souls, but now they have none. Their minds seem to be darkened, and they cannot see spiritual things, as they have done in times past. Formerly, when they read the Scriptures, they used often to have light come in, and they seemed to have an understanding and relish for what they read, and were filled with comfort. But now when they read, it is all a dead letter, and they have no taste for it, and are obliged to force themselves to read; they seem to have no pleasure in it, but it is a mere task and burden. Formerly they used to have passages of Scripture come to their minds when they were not reading, which brought much light and sweetness with them. But now they have none. Formerly they used to feel the sweet exercises of grace. They could trust in God, and could find a spirit of resignation to his will, and had love drawn forth, and sweet longings after God and Christ, and a sweet complacence in God; but now they are dull and dead. Formerly they used to meet with God in the ordinances of his house: it was sweet to sit and hear the Word preached, and it seemed to bring light and life with it; they used to feel life and sweetness in public prayers, and their hearts were elevated in singing God's praises. But now it is otherwise. Formerly they used to delight in the duty of prayer: the time which they spent in their closet between God and their own souls was sweet to them. But now when they go thither, they do not meet God; and they take no delight in drawing near to God in their closets. When they do pray, it seems to be a mere lifeless, heartless performance. They utter such and such words, but they seem to be nothing but words; their hearts are not engaged. Their minds are continually wandering and going to and fro after one vanity and another. With this decay of the exercise of grace their hope greatly decays; and the evidences of their piety are exceedingly clouded. When they look into their hearts, it seems to them that they can see nothing there from which they should hope; and when they consider after what manner they live, it seems to them to argue that they have no grace. They have but little of anything which is new to furnish comfortable evidence to them of their good estate; and as to their old evidences, they are greatly darkened. Their former experience, in which they took great comfort, looks dim, and a great way off, and out of sight to them. They have almost forgotten it, and have no pleasure in thinking or speaking of it.

And sometimes true Christians are brought into terrible distress. They are not only deprived of their former comforts and have their former hope obscured, but they have inward distressing darkness. God does not only hide his face, but they have a sense of his anger. He seems to frown upon them. So it appears to have been with David: "Deep calleth unto deep at the noise of thy waterspouts; all thy waves and thy billows are gone over me" (Ps. 42:7). So also with Heman: "Thou hast laid me in the lowest pit, in darkness, in the deeps. Thy wrath lieth hard upon me, and thou hast afflicted me with all thy waves" (Ps. 88:6–7).

SIN THE CAUSE OF DARKNESS

It is sin which is the occasion of this trouble and darkness. Whenever the godly meet with such darkness, there is some Achan in their souls which is the occasion of all this; and this is sin. This is the occasion of the darkness of the godly, as well as the troubles which natural men have under awakenings. It is not for want of love in God toward his saints, or readiness to grant comfort to them; neither is God's hand shortened that it cannot save, nor his ear heavy that he cannot hear. It is their sin which hides God's face from them (Isa. 59:1–2). Sin is the occasion of this darkness of the saints, in these three ways.

Because of the strength of remaining corruption

Sometimes it is owing to the weakness and small degree of grace infused in conversion, and the strength of remaining corruption. The work of God is the same in all who are converted, so far that their sin is mortified and that which reigned before does not reign now. The heart is changed from darkness to light, and from death to life, and turned from sin to God. And yet the work is very different with respect to the degree of the mortification of sin, and the degree of grace which is infused. Some have more spiritual light given in their first conversion than others; have greater discoveries, and are brought at once to a much greater acquaintance with God, and have their hearts more humbled, and more weaned from sin and the world, and more filled with the love of God and Christ, and are brought nearer to heaven than others. Some at first conversion have a much more eminent work of grace in their hearts than others. Some have emphatically but little grace infused, and consequently their corruptions are left in much greater strength: when it is so, it is no wonder that such have a weaker hope, and less light and comfort than others. The natural tendency of indwelling sin in the saints is to cloud and darken the mind; and therefore, the more of it remains, the more will it have this effect. Persons can know their own good estate in no other way than by seeking or perceiving grace in their hearts. But certainly the less of it there is, with the more difficulty will it be seen or felt. As indwelling sin prevails, so does it the more obscure and cloud grace, as a great smoke clouds and hides a spark. And therefore the more there is of this indwelling sin, the more will grace be hid. The greater the strength in which corruption is left, the more rare will be the good frames which the godly have, and the more frequent and of longer continuance will be their times of darkness.

It may be the darkness with which the saints meet is from some particular corruption, which has always hitherto been in too great prevalence and strength, and has never yet been mortified to such a degree but that it continues a great troubler in the soul. Grace being weak, the sin of the constitution takes advantage, whether that be a proud and haughty temper, or a covetous spirit, or an addictedness to some sensuality, or a peevish, fretful, discontented spirit, or ill temper, or a quarrelsome spirit, or disposition to high resentment. Or whether it be any other corrupt disposition, which is the sin to which they are chiefly exposed by natural temper, or by their education and former custom. If the grace which is infused at conversion be comparatively weak, this constitutional sin will take the advantage, and will dreadfully cloud the mind, and hinder spiritual comfort, and bring trouble and darkness.

There is a great variety in the work of grace upon men's hearts as to the particular discoveries which are then given, and the particular graces which are in chief exercise; whereby it comes to pass that some in their conversion are more assisted against one corruption and others against another. Some in their conversion, as well as in the manner of their experience from time to time, have more of the exercise of one grace, and others more sensible exercises of another. And whatever that grace be of which they have the most lively exercises, they are thereby most assisted against that particular corruption which is its opposite. Hence some particular corruptions may be left in much greater prevalence than others, and so be a greater occasion of darkness. Thus some, in the particular exercises which they have, may not be so especially assisted against pride as others, whereby their pride may take occasion to work. And when they have had spiritual discoveries and comfort, they may be lifted up with them. And this may be an occasion of displeasing and grieving his Holy Spirit, and so of their having a great deal of darkness. They may not have seen so much of their own emptiness as some others, and so their corruption may work much more by self-confidence than others; and no wonder that self-confident persons meet with darkness. No wonder that, when men trust in themselves for light and grace, their confidence fails, and they go without that for which they trusted in themselves.

Because of gross transgression

Sometimes the saints are in great darkness on occasion of some gross transgression into which they have fallen. So it was with David, when he fell into gross sin in the matter of Uriah. He exceedingly quenched the influences of the Spirit of God by it, and God withdrew those influences from him, and the comforts which they had imparted; as appears by his earnestly praying for their restoration: "Restore unto me the joy of my salvation, and uphold me with thy free Spirit" (Ps. 51:12). When Christians fall into gross transgression, it is commonly the fact that an exceedingly deep darkness follows.

Because of corrupt habits

When they do not fall into any particular gross and scandalous transgression, yet they sometimes exceedingly darken their minds by corrupt frames and evil habits into which they fall. There is much remaining corruption in the hearts of Christians, and oftentimes they get into very ill frames. Some particular corruptions grow very prevalent. Sometimes they grow proud and conceited of themselves, either on account of their own godliness and the good opinion others have of them, or on some other account. Sometimes they fall into a worldly frame, and spiritual things grow more tasteless to them, and their hearts are desperately bent on the acquisition of worldly good. Sometimes their minds grow light and vain, and their affections are wholly fixed on the vanities of youth, on dress, and gaiety, and fashion.

Some, because their minds are not occupied as once they were with spiritual enjoyments and delights—sweetly meditating on heavenly things, breathing and longing after them, and earnestly seeking them—become the slaves of their sensual appetites. Others grow contentious and quarrelsome, are often angry with those around them, and cherish habitual rancor against them in their hearts. They become willful and obstinate, and stir up strife, and oppose others with vehemence, determining at all hazards to carry their own measures, and delighting to have those who oppose them defeated and humbled. It hurts them to have others prosper. Their minds and hearts are full of turmoil and heat and vehemence against one and another. Others fall into a discontented, fretful, and impatient frame at the disposals of Providence. And oftentimes many of these things go together. And as these persons sink into such unhappy frames in their hearts, so they pursue very sinful courses of conduct. They behave themselves unsuitably, so as to dishonor God, and greatly to wound religion. They do not appear to others to savor of a good spirit. They fall into the practice of allowing themselves too great liberties in indulging their sensual appetites, in the gratification of covetousness and pride, in strife, in backbiting, and a violent pursuit after the world. They slide into those corrupt frames and evil ways by means of their first giving way to a slothful spirit. They are not so diligent and earnest in religion as they once were, but indulge their slothful disposition, and discontinue their watch, and so lie open to temptation. Thus ill frames imperceptibly creep upon them, and they insensibly more and more fall into sinful practices. So it was with David. Their sin, into which they fall in consequence of this degenerate and sinful state of the affections and the life, is the occasion of a great deal of darkness. God withdraws his Spirit from them, their light goes out, and the evidences of their piety grow dim and obscure. They seem to be in a great measure as they were before they were converted, and they have no sensible communion with God. Thus sin is the occasion of trouble and darkness to the Christian.

GOD RETURNS COMFORT AND HOPE[1]

When the saints are in darkness, their darkness is not perpetual, but God will restore hope and comfort to them again. When one of Christ's sheep wanders away and gets into the wilderness, Christ the good Shepherd will not leave him in the wilderness, but will seek him, and will lay him on his shoulders, and bring him home again. We cannot tell how long God may leave his saints in the dark, but yet surely their darkness shall not last forever; for light is sown to the righteous, and gladness to the upright in heart

---

1. In the Hickman edition of Edwards's works, this section (beginning with "When the saints are in darkness") and the next one here (beginning with "When it is thus with Christians") are reversed. They were correctly numbered in Hickman according to the outline Edwards provided for this section, but mistakenly placed in the sequence 2, 4, 3, 5. Very likely, during the publication of the Hickman volumes, the order of Edwards's third and fourth points was confused, owing to his three similarly numbered subpoints under 2, which led to the expectation that 4 should come next. I have restored the order of sections in conformity to Edwards's outline.

(Ps. 97:11). God, in the covenant of grace in which they have an interest, has promised them joy and comfort; he has promised them everlasting joy (Isa. 61:7). Satan may be suffered for a time to bring them into darkness, but they shall be brought out again. God may be provoked to hide his face from them for a time; and if it seems long, yet it is indeed but a little time: "For a small moment have I forsaken thee; but with great mercies I will gather thee. In a little wrath I hid my face from thee for a moment; but with everlasting kindness will I have mercy on thee" (Isa. 54:7–8). And: "Weeping may endure for a night, but joy cometh in the morning" (Ps. 30:5).

TROUBLE INCREASED BEFORE HOPE REVIVES

When it is thus with Christians, their trouble is commonly greatly increased a little before the renewal of hope and comfort. When sin prevails, as has been said, in the hearts of Christians, they are not wont to be easy and quiet like secure sinners. There is commonly more or less of an inward struggling and uneasiness. Grace in the heart, though it be dreadfully oppressed, and, as it were, overwhelmed, yet will be resisting its enemy and struggling for liberty. So that it is not with Christians, in their ill frames and under the prevalence of corruption, altogether as it is with carnal, wicked men, who are secure. And there is this good reason for it, that the former have a principle of spiritual life in their souls, which the latter have not.

Yet Christians in their ill frames may fall into a great deal of security and senselessness; for sin is of a stupefying nature and, wherever it prevails, will have more or less of that effect. When they fall into a sinful, worldly, proud, or contentious frame, they are wont to have a great degree of senselessness and stupidity with it. And especially when they fall into gross sins has it a tendency greatly to stupefy the soul. It obviously had this effect on David. He seems to have been strangely stupefied when Nathan came to him with the parable of the rich man who injuriously took the poor man's ewe lamb from him. He was enraged with the man in the parable, but did not seem to reflect on himself, or think how parallel his case was with this. And while they are thus senseless, their trouble is not so great; and if they feel the weight of sin it is not so burdensome to them.

But God is wont, before he renews comfort and hope to them, to bring them into greater trouble. As a sinner before his first comfort in his conversion is brought into trouble, so it is wont to be with the saints after their backslidings and decays, before renewed hope and comfort is granted. There is a work of awakening wrought upon them. While they remain in their corrupt frames, they are, as it were, asleep. They are like the ten foolish virgins who slumbered and slept; and as persons who are asleep, they are unconscious, not sensible where they are, nor what are their circumstances. Therefore when God is coming and returning to them by his Spirit, commonly his first work upon them is a work of awakening, to wake them out of sleep, and rouse them to some sensibility, to make them sensible of the great folly of their ways, and how they have displeased and offended God, and what mischief they have done. But yet it is really much better with them now than before they began to come to themselves. Their circumstances are much more eligible and more hopeful, though sometimes they are in distress almost insupportable. And a little before God renews light and comfort, they have a very great sense of God's anger, and his wrath lies heavy upon them. So it seems to have been with David a little before the restoration of spiritual comfort to him, which made him speak of the bones which God had broken, when he was praying for the renewal of comfort: "Make me to hear joy and gladness, that the bones which thou hast broken may rejoice" (Ps. 51:8). And probably he has respect to the same thing in Psalm 38, which he calls his psalm to bring remembrance: "Thine arrows stick fast in me, and thy hand presseth me sore. There is no soundness in my flesh, because of thine anger; neither is there any rest in my bones, because of my sin. For mine iniquities have gone over mine head; as an heavy burden they are too heavy for me" (Ps. 38:2–4).

And often when God is about to bring them to themselves, and to restore comfort to them, he first brings them into some very great and sore temporal calamity and trouble, and awakens them by that, and in this first brings them into the wilderness before he speaks comfortably to them:

Then he openeth the ears of men, and sealeth their instruction, that he may withdraw man from his purpose, and hide pride from man. He keepeth back his soul from the pit, and his life from perishing by the sword. He is chastened also with pain upon his bed, and the multitude of his bones with strong pain; so that his life abhorreth bread, and his soul dainty meat. His flesh is consumed away, that it cannot be seen; and his bones, that were not seen, stick out. Yea, his soul draweth near unto the grave, and his life to the destroyers. If there be a messenger with him, and interpreter, one among a thousand, to show man his uprightness, then he is gracious unto him, and saith, "Deliver him from going down to the pit; I have found a ransom." His flesh shall be fresher than a child's; he shall return to the days of his youth. He shall pray unto God, and he shall be favorable unto him, and he shall see his face with joy; for he will render unto man his righteousness. He looketh upon men, and if any say, "I have sinned, and perverted that which was right, and it profited me not," he will deliver his soul from going into the pit, and his life shall see the light. Lo, all these things worketh God, oftentimes with man, to bring back his soul from the pit, to be enlightened with the light of the living. (Job 33:16-30)

Thus those who are very weak in grace sometimes meet with great and sore trouble, both of body and mind, which is an occasion of a new work, as it were, of grace upon their hearts; so that they are more eminent saints afterwards, and have much more comfort.

HOPE AND COMFORT RENEWED ON THE SLAYING OF THE TROUBLER

Hope and comfort are renewed to them on the slaying of the troubler. All sin is truly mortified in conversion, or has its death-wounds then. And all the exercises of it afterwards are, in some respects, as the efforts and strugglings of a dying enemy. But yet all life is not actually extinct, and therefore it needs to be further mortified, to receive more deadly wounds. Sin is slain in the godly after trouble and darkness, and before the renewing of comfort in these three ways.

Three ways sin is slain

1. It is slain as to the former degrees of it. All remains of corruption are not extirpated. Sin does not cease to be in the heart; but it ceases to be any more in such strength as it has been; it ceases to have that prevalence.

2. It is slain as to the former ways of exercise. The former ways of sin are forsaken. They are further afterwards from such ways of sin than ever before. The heart is fortified against them. Thus if a godly man has been in a way of contention and strife, when he comes to himself again, he slays his contention; he kills sin as to that way of exercising it. Or if it be some way of sensuality, when he comes to himself, he will slay his sensuality, and cast it out from him.

3. It is totally and perfectly slain in his will and inclination. There is that renewed opposition made against it, which implies a mortal inclination and design against it. What the saint seeks when he comes to himself after a time of great declension, is to be the death of sin, which has been so prevalent in him, and perfectly to extirpate it. He acts in what he does as a mortal enemy; and if he does not perfectly destroy it at one blow, it is not for want of inclination, but for want of strength. The godly man does not deal mercifully and tenderly with sin, but as far as in him lies, he deals with it as the children of Israel dealt with Achan, as it were, stones it with stones, and burns it with fire with all which belongs to it. They do not at all spare it, as wicked men do; they aim at the very life, and nothing short of it.

Implications of the slaying of sin

The saints' slaying of the troubler after great backslidings and ill frames implies the following things.

1. There is a conviction of the evil of their sin. They are brought to consideration. They think on their ways before they turn their feet (Ps. 119:59). They consider how they have behaved themselves, how unworthily, how unfaithful they have been to their profession, how ungratefully, and disagreeably to the mercies they have received. They consider how they have provoked God, and have deserved his wrath. They find the troubler led them to see a great deal more of the sinfulness and corruption of their hearts commonly than before. In this respect the work of God with saints after great declinings is agree-

able to his work in the heart of a natural man in order to his conversion.

2. There is a gracious humiliation of soul before God for it. The gracious soul, when convinced of sin after great declensions, and recovered out of them, is deeply humbled; for it is brought to the dust before God. There is an evangelical repentance; the heart is broken for sin. That sacrifice is offered to God which David offered rather than burnt offerings after his great fall: "For thou desirest not sacrifice, else would I give it; thou delightest not in burnt offering. The sacrifices of God are a broken spirit; a broken and a contrite heart, O God, thou wilt not despise" (Ps. 51:16–17). They are brought as Job was, after he had sinned in complaining of God's dealings with him, to abhor themselves (Job 42:6). And they are in a meeker frame, as the Christian Corinthians were, after they had greatly gone out of the way and had been reproved by the apostle Paul: "For behold the self-same thing, that ye sorrowed after a godly sort, what carefulness it wrought in you, yea what clearing of yourselves, yea what indignation, yea what fear, yea what vehement desire, yea what zeal, yea what revenge" (2 Cor. 7:11). They were filled with sorrow, and with a kind of indignation, zeal, and spirit of revenge against themselves for their folly and so ungratefully treating God. When Christians are convinced of their sin after remarkable miscarriages and ill frames, they are commonly convinced of many of the same things of which they were convinced under their first humiliation, but to a greater degree than ever before. They are brought under new con-

viction, and a greater conviction than ever before, of their own emptiness, and what sinful, vile, utterly unworthy creatures they are; how undeserving they are of any mercy, and how much they deserve God's wrath. And this conviction works by a gracious humbling of the soul. The grace of humility is greatly increased by it, and very commonly they are more poor in spirit and lowly of heart during all their future life. They see more what cause there is for them to lay their hands on their mouths, and to walk humbly with God, and lie low before him.

3. There is a renewed application to Christ as a Savior from sin. There is a renewed act of reliance on him for justification, of faith in his blood to cleanse them, and of trust in his righteousness to cover their nakedness and filthiness. And Christ as a Savior becomes more precious to them. As they have a greater sense of their own emptiness and vileness, so they have a more entire dependence on Christ's fullness.

4. The heart is farther separated from those ways of sin, and more confirmed against them, than ever. After it they commonly have a greater dread of it, and greater abhorrence, look upon it more as an enemy, and remember what they have suffered from it; and their hearts are more confirmed against it than ever. They have stronger resolutions to all which savors of the like, and all which might lead to it. Therefore this is mentioned among the effects of the repentance of the Corinthians after their going astray: "What carefulness it wrought in you, yea what clearing of yourselves, yea what fear, yea what earnest desire." There was a more than ordinary fear

and dread of the like sin for the future, and more carefulness
to shun it, and a more earnest desire of the contrary.

The return of hope and comfort

The work of God in the heart of a saint after declension oftentimes, in many respects, resembles the work of
God in a sinner at his conversion; though it is not in all
respects like it because of the great difference in the subject. When the troubler comes thus to be slain after times
of trouble and darkness in the godly, then God is wont to
open a door of hope. The darkness which has covered them,
which was greatest a little before, is now scattered, and
light arises. It may be before there had been a long night of
clouds and darkness. But now the clouds begin to scatter,
and the sweet refreshing beams begin to break forth and
come down into the heart. The soul, which has been
wounded, is now healed. God pours in the oil of comfort.
The renewed sense which is given of Christ's fullness and
sufficiency gives new life and hope and joy. The troubler
being slain, God now grants renewed discoveries of his
glory, and renewed manifestations of his grace; and the
soul, which was before in darkness, is now entertained with
sweet views. And now that hope, which was so weakened
and was almost ready to fail, is revived, and greatly confirmed. Now the soul is enabled to take comfort in the
promises. Now the saint sees evidences of his own good
estate by the renewed manifestations which God makes of
himself, and renewed exercises of grace.

Before the soul was greatly exercised with doubts and fears and dark clouds; and much time was spent in reviewing past experiences, and looking over and examining those things which were formerly regarded as evidences of piety; and all in vain. They pored on past experiences, but to no satisfaction. And the reason was, the troubler was not slain, but remained alive. But now God gives them new light and new experiences, which in a few moments do more toward scattering their clouds and removing their fears than all their poring on past experiences could do for months, and probably for years. Before their hearts seemed in a great measure dead as to spiritual exercises. But now there is, as it were, new life. Now when they read the Scripture, and when they hear the Word preached, it is with a savor and relish of it. Now they can find God in his Word and ordinances. Now Christ comes to them, and manifests himself to them, and they are admitted again to communion with God. When Christians have comfort and hope thus renewed, their comforts are commonly purer than ever. Their joys are more humble joys, freer from any mixture and taint of self-righteousness, than before.

STUDY QUESTIONS

1. According to Edwards, how might a believer be able to tell when he or she had departed the path of holiness and was beginning to stray into the "wilderness" of sin? What is it like to experience such darkness? How is it expressed?

2. What reasons does Edwards give, in the second section of this chapter, for why sin makes such inroads in our lives? How might a Christian prepare himself or herself to avoid these pitfalls?

3. Suppose you knew a believer who had strayed into the wilderness and seemed no longer interested in pursuing holiness in the Lord. How would you be able to tell that this was so? How might you approach such a person to help him or her begin to seek renewed hope and comfort in the Lord?

4. Summarize Edwards's thoughts about how we ought to deal with the lingering sin in our lives. Why is this an important part of the pursuit of holiness?

5. Re-read the last section of this chapter, headed "The return of hope and comfort." Have you ever experienced this? What were you experiencing before this? Why? What did the Lord use to lead you out of the wilderness? How did you deal with sin? What did you learn as a result of this experience?

❖ *Chapter 10* ❖

REASONS FOR THIS DOCTRINE

Ever the careful theologian, Edwards now takes us into a considera-
tion of the reasons why God does this—why he leads his people into
times of trouble when sin has entered their lives, before he restores them
to hope and comfort again. Edwards gives three reasons why we must
wander in the wilderness at such times, and three reasons why sin
must first be slain before hope and comfort are renewed.

Having thus shown that God is wont to cause hope and
comfort to arise to the soul after trouble and humbling for
sin, and upon slaying the troubler, both at first conversion
and afterwards, I would now give the reasons of the doctrine.

WHY THE WILDERNESS

I would show why God is wont to give comfort after
trouble and humbling for sin; or why he is wont to bring
the soul into the wilderness before he speaks comfortably
to it, and leads it into the valley of Achor before he opens
a door of hope.

For the preparation of the soul

It is that the soul may be prepared for a confiding application of itself to Christ for comfort. It is the will of God that men should have true hope and comfort conferred upon them in no other way than by Jesus Christ. It is only by him that sinners have comfort at their conversion; and it is by him only that the saints have renewed hope and comfort after their declensions. And therefore the way to obtain this comfort is to look to him, to fly for refuge to him. And in order to this, persons have need to be brought to a sense of their necessity of him. And that they may be so, it is needful that they should be sensible of their calamity and misery, that they should be in trouble, and be brought to see their utter helplessness in themselves. And not only natural men, but Christians also, who are fallen into sin and are in a dead and senseless frame, need something to make them more sensible of their necessity of Christ. Indeed the best are not so sensible of their need of Christ but that they need to be made more sensible; but especially those who are in ill and dead frames and a declining state need trouble and humbling to make them sensible of their need of Christ, and to prepare their minds for a renewed confiding application to Christ as their only remedy. The godly in such a case are sick with a sore disease, and Christ is the only Physician who can heal them; and they need to be sensible of their disease, that they may see their need of a physician. They, as well as natural men, need to be in a storm and tempest to make them sensible of their need to fly to him who is a hiding place from the wind, and a covert from the tempest.

A Christian who wanders away from God is like Noah's dove, which flew from the ark. She flew about till weary and spent, seeking rest somewhere else, but found no rest for the sole of her foot, and then she returned to the ark. So it is needful that the soul of the godly man who wanders from Christ should become weary, and find no rest for the sole of his foot, that so he may see his need of returning to Christ. Therefore it is said concerning the children of Israel in Hosea 2:6, "Therefore, behold, I will hedge up thy way with thorns, and make a wall that she shall not find her paths." And in our context, "She shall follow after her lovers, but she shall not overtake them; and she shall seek them, but shall not find them. Then shall she say, 'I will go and return to my first husband, for then it was better with me than now'" (Hos. 2:7). When gracious souls wander from Christ, their husband, following after other lovers, God is wont to bring them into trouble and distress, and make them see that their other lovers cannot help them, that so they may see that it is best for them to return to their first husband.

That comfort and hope may be more prized

Another end of God in it is that comfort and hope may be the more prized when obtained. We see in temporal things that the worth and value of any enjoyment is learned by the want of it. He who is sick knows the worth of health. He who is in pain knows how to prize ease. He who is in a storm at sea knows how to prize safety on shore. And people who are subject to the grievances of war know how to value peace. He who endures hardships of captivity and slavery is thereby taught how to value liberty. And so it is in spiritual things. He who is brought to see his misery in being without hope is prepared to prize hope when obtained. He who is brought into distress through fear of hell and God's wrath is the more prepared to prize the comfort which arises from the manifestation of the favor of God, and a sense of safety from hell. He who is brought to see his utter emptiness and extreme poverty and necessity, and his perishing condition on that account, is thoroughly prepared to prize and rejoice in the manifestation of a fullness in Christ. And those godly persons who are fallen into corrupt and senseless frames greatly stand in need of something to make them more sensible of their want of spiritual comfort and hope. Their living as they do shows that they have too little sense of the worth and value of that comfort, and those inestimable spiritual and saving blessings which God has bestowed upon them; otherwise they never would deal so ungratefully with God, who has bestowed them. If they did not greatly err in slighting spiritual comfort, as the children of Israel did manna, their hearts would never, to such a degree, have gone out after vanity and earthly enjoyments and carnal delights. They need to be brought into trouble and darkness to make them sensible of the worth of hope and comfort, and to teach them to prize it. They need to be brought into the wilderness and left for a time to wander and suffer hunger and thirst in a barren desert to teach them how to prize their vineyards. A sense of the pardon of sin and the favor of God, and a hope of eternal life, do not afford comfort and joy to the soul any farther than they are valued and prized. So that the trouble and darkness which go before comfort serve to render the joy and comfort the greater when obtained, and so are in mercy to those for whom God intends comfort.

To acknowledge divine power and grace

It is so ordered that divine power and grace may be acknowledged in giving hope and comfort. There is naturally in men an exceeding insensibility of their dependence on God and a great disposition to ascribe those things which they enjoy to themselves or to second causes. This disposition reigns in natural men. They are wholly under the power of it. Therefore they need to be taught their own helplessness and utter insufficiency and utter unworthiness. Otherwise, if hope and comfort should be bestowed upon them, they would surely ascribe all to themselves, or the creature, and be lifted up by it, and would not give God the glory. Therefore it is God's manner first to humble sinners before he comforts them.

And all this self-confident disposition is not extirpated out of the hearts of the godly, and especially when they get into ill frames does it prevail. And it is very requisite that, before any remarkable comfort is bestowed upon them, they should be the subjects of renewed humbling. They need renewedly to see what helpless creatures they are, that so, when light is bestowed, they may be sensible how it is owing to God and not to themselves or any other; and that they may, by their troubles and humblings, be prepared the more to admire God's power and mercy, and free and rich grace to them. While men are continued in fullness in a fruitful land, they will not learn their own helplessness; and therefore God will cast them out of this fullness into a wilderness. This is plainly intimated to be the reason of God's so dealing with the children of Israel, as is said in the text. The church of Israel, before God thus led her into the wilderness, did not ascribe her comforts to God, as in the eighth verse: "For she did not know that I gave her corn, and wine, and oil, and multiplied her silver and gold." But they ascribed them to her idols. Similarly, in verse 5: "For she said, I will go after my lovers, that give me my bread and my water, my wool and my flax, mine oil and my drink." And in verse 12, "These are my rewards, that my lovers have given me." For this reason it is that God takes away those things, as in verse 9: "Therefore will I return and take away my corn in the time thereof, and my wine in the season thereof, and will recover my wool and my flax given to cover her nakedness." And in verses 11 and 12: "I will also cause all her mirth to cease, her feast days, her new moons, and her Sabbaths, and all her solemn feasts. And I will destroy her vines and her fig trees, whereof she hath said, 'These are my rewards that my lovers have given me'; and I will make them a forest, and the beasts of the field shall eat them." God took them away and turned her vineyards into a forest, and made her sensible that they were from him; and then he restored them again.

For these reasons God is wont to bring souls into trouble, and to humble them for sin before he comforts them.

Why the Troubler Must First Be Slain

I proceed to give the reasons why hope and comfort are not obtained till sin, which is the troubler, is slain.

Sin God's mortal enemy

While sin is harbored and preserved alive, it tends to provoke God to frown and express his anger. Sin is God's mortal enemy. It is that which his soul infinitely hates and to which he is an irreconcilable enemy. And therefore if we harbor this, and suffer it to live in our hearts and to govern our practice, we can expect no other than that it will provoke God's frowns. Spiritual comfort consists in the manifestations of God's favor and friendly communion with God. But how can we expect this at the same time that we harbor his mortal enemy? We see what God said to Joshua while Achan was alive: "Neither will I be with you any more, except ye destroy the accursed thing from among you" (Josh. 7:12).

Sin prevents the exercises of grace

The natural tendency of sin is to darken the mind and trouble the conscience. There is nothing which wounds a well-informed conscience but sin. Sin is the enemy of grace, and therefore the natural tendency of it is to oppose and keep down the exercises of grace, and so to extinguish spiritual comfort; for spiritual comfort comes in no other way than by the exercises of grace. That which prevents the exercises of grace darkens the evidences of a man's good estate. For there are no evidences of this but the exercises of grace. Sin does as much tend to keep out spiritual comfort as clouds tend to hide the light of the sun. And therefore it is necessary that this should be removed in order to our receiving light and comfort. It is impossible in its own nature that any should have spiritual light and comfort before sin is mortified. If sinners had comfort while sin is reigning in power, it could not be spiritual comfort; for spiritual comfort is the same with gracious comfort. But how can there be gracious comfort where grace has no place? But if there be grace, sin will not be reigning in power; for the nature of grace is to mortify sin. And as there can be no spiritual comfort without a degree of mortification of sin in those in whom sin is mortified, spiritual comfort cannot be any more than in proportion as sin is mortified.

To keep from abusing the hope of eternal life

A hope of eternal life, if given before the slaying of sin, would be misimproved and abused. If it were possible that a sinner could obtain a title to eternal life before sin was mortified, and so could have his own safety and God's favor manifested to him, he would only improve it to encourage and embolden himself in sin. Hope, if they had it then, would have a pernicious influence and tendency. Till sin is slain, they stand in need of fear to restrain sin. If fear were once gone before sin is slain, they would soon run into all manner of wickedness, and without restraint. And so Christians themselves, while they are in corrupt frames, stand in need of fear to restrain sin; for at such times love is in a great degree dormant. It is of necessity that persons should have some principle or other to restrain them from sin. But there is no principle which can be effectual to restrain men any farther than it is in exercise. If love is not in exercise it will not restrain men, so that at such times the saints need fear. And therefore God has wisely ordered it, that at such times their evidences should be darkened and their hopes clouded, that they may have fear, when love is not awake, to restrain them. The godly themselves, if their hope were all alive at those times when they are in carnal and thoughtless frames and grace is asleep, would be in great danger to abuse their hope and take encouragement from it to indulge their lusts, or at least, to be the less careful to restrain and resist them. For we see that, in such frames, though their hopes are clouded and they have a considerable degree of fear, yet they are careless and negligent. But how much more so would they be if they had no fear to restrain them!

STUDY QUESTIONS

1. Jonathan Edwards believed that it was important to understand, as far as one is able—that is, as far as the Scriptures explain—why God does the things he does. See if you can summarize the reasons for God's leading his

people to trouble before he restores them to hope and comfort. First, why is it necessary for the saints to experience a "season in the wilderness" when they have begun to leave off the pursuit of holiness (three reasons)?

2. Next, why is it necessary for sin, the "troubler of the soul," to be utterly slain before hope and comfort revive, and the journey toward holiness can resume (three reasons)?

3. Suppose you have a friend, a believer, who calls you and wants to talk. She says she has been troubled and depressed of late, and that she seems far away from God. She has begun to doubt her salvation and is afraid that God has given up on her. What are some questions you might ask this person to help her understand where she is, why she is there, and what she must do in order to get back on the path of hope and comfort?

4. Knowing what you know about how sin, finding a harbor in our souls, can lead us off the path of the pursuit of holiness and into the wilderness of darkness and trouble, what can you do to help ensure that this doesn't happen to you? Or that, if it does, you catch it early on, and take the necessary steps (such as those you outlined in question 3 above)?

5. Review the goals you set for yourself at the end of chapter I. Are you making progress? Are you beginning to understand God's gracious work of sanctification any better, as well as what he requires of us as we pursue holiness in the Lord? In what ways?

❊ *Chapter 11* ❊

APPLICATION OF
THE DOCTRINE

*Edwards now proceeds to his application, in which he shows how the
doctrine he has been developing—of trouble coming before hope and
comfort—leads us to extol the wisdom of God. By examining our
present hope and comfort—whether it is true or false—and by following the directions of Scripture in rooting out the troubler of our
souls, we may recover the path that leads to the pursuit of holiness and
blessedness in the Lord.*

USE OF INSTRUCTION

The wonderful wisdom of God

Hence we may observe the wonderful wisdom of God
in his dealings with the souls of men. When we consider
what has been said, with the reasons of it, we may see just
cause to admire the divine wisdom in his ordinary dealings
with respect to those for whom he intends comfort. His
wisdom is admirable in his dealings *with natural men* in fitting and preparing them for comfort, in bringing them

into such troubles and distress, and hedging up their way with thorns—as is expressed in the context—and leaving them in their distress to follow after their lovers, their idols, without being able to overtake them; in taking away their vineyards, and all those things in which they trusted, and making them a forest; and so showing them what poor, destitute, helpless creatures they are, before he gives them comfort.

And so we may well admire the divine wisdom in his method of dealing *with his saints* who decline and fall into sin, or get into corrupt frames and ill ways. God knows how to order things concerning them; and there is marvelous wisdom observable in his manner of dealing with them in such cases. We may well admire how wisely God orders things in what has been said, for his own glory, to secure the glory due to his power and free grace, and to bring men to a sense of their dependence on him, and to ascribe all to him. And how he orders things for the glory of his Son, that he may have all the glory of the salvation of men, who is worthy of it, in that he laid down his life for their salvation. And also how wisely God orders things for the good of his own elect people, how he brings good out of evil, and light out of darkness. How wisely he consults their good and comfort in those things which appear to them to be most against them. How he wisely prepares them for good and makes way for their receiving comfort, and for its being the more sweet, the more prized and delighted in, when it is obtained. And oftentimes in bringing about this in those things which they think at the time to be signs of God's hatred. And how wisely God orders things for preventing men's abusing a sense of their own safety, to giving the reins to their lusts. It is ordered so that, at those times when sin prevails and there would be danger of this, the evidences of their safety are hid from their eyes, and the fear of hell comes on to keep them in awe; and that hope and comfort should be given only at such times and in such manner that they should have influence to draw men off from sin, and to prompt them to diligence in duty and the service of God; and that when it would have most of this tendency, then they should have most of it.

When we consider these things, we may well cry out with the apostle, "O the depth both of wisdom and knowledge of God! How unsearchable are his judgments, and his ways past finding out!" (Rom. 11:33).

Cause for encouragement

Hence we may learn that souls who are in darkness, and, as it were, in a wilderness, have no cause to be discouraged. For by the doctrine we learn that this is the way, often, in order to hope and comfort. Persons are very often ready to be discouraged by this. God seems to frown. They have a sense of his anger. They cry to him, and he does not seem to hear their prayers. They have been striving for relief, but it seems to be to no purpose. They are in such circumstances that everything looks dark; everything seems to be against them. They are lost in a wilderness; they cannot find the way out. They have gone round and round and returned again to the same place. They know not which way to turn themselves, or what to do. Their hearts are ready to sink.

But you may gather encouragement from this doctrine; for by it you may learn that you have no cause to despair. For it is frequently God's manner to bring persons into such circumstances in order to prepare them for hope and comfort. The children of Israel were ready to be discouraged at the Red Sea, when they saw Pharaoh and the hosts pursuing them. But it was only to prepare them for greater joy after their deliverance. Joshua and the hosts of Israel were ready to be discouraged when they were smitten at Ai, as you may see in Josh. 7, etc. So that you, who are in the wilderness, may take encouragement from hence, still earnestly seek to God, and hope for light and comfort in his time.

Use of Self-examination

By this persons may try their hopes and comforts, whether they are of the right kind. If they are such as have arisen after the manner as is spoken of in the doctrine; if it is a hope which you found in the valley of Achor, in the sense which has been explained; it is a sign that it is a hope which God has given you, and so a hope which you are not to cast away, but which you are to retain and rejoice in, and bless God for it. Therefore particularly inquire concerning your hopes and comforts, whether they have arisen in your souls when humbled for sin, and in the slaying of sin.

Examine whether hope and comfort are from humbling for sin

Inquire whether your hopes and comforts have been given you upon your soul's being humbled for sin. You may try this by three things.

1. Whether you have seen what a miserable, helpless creature you were. When your hopes and comforts have arisen in your heart, has it been upon your soul's receiving such a sight of yourself; or has your hope been accompanied with such a sense of soul? When hope was given *at first*, was it implanted in a heart thus prepared? And when you have had remarkable comfort and joy from time to time, has your joy been accompanied with such a sense and frame of mind? At the same time that you have had a strong hope of God's favor, and that Christ was yours, have you been nothing in your own eyes; have you at such times appeared to yourself to be a poor, little, helpless, unworthy creature, deserving nothing at the hands of God?

And do not only inquire whether in your own apprehension you had some such sight of yourself at first, before your comfort. If you ever had a right understanding of yourself, of your own heart and your own state, you will never lose it. It will revive from time to time. If you had it when you received your first comfort, the same sense will come again; when your comforts are revived, this will revive with them. If the first joy was granted to a heart thus prepared, there will *from time to time* be a sense of your own emptiness and worthlessness, arising with your joys and comforts. It will be a deep sense of what a poor, miserable, and exceedingly sinful creature you are. True comfort is wont to come in such a manner. There is usually a self-emptying, a soul-abasing sense of heart accompanying it. So that, at the same time that God lifts up the soul with comfort and joy and inward sweetness, he casts it down with abasement. Evangelical and gracious humiliation and spiritual comfort are companions which go one with the other and keep company together. When one comes, the other is wont to come with it.

It is not wont to be so with *false hopes and comforts*. But pride and self-fullness are wont to be the companions of false comfort. Indeed, there may be a counterfeit abasement going with it. But if you examine it, you will find that that very seeming abasement or humiliation lifts the man up and fills him full of himself. The hypocrite, in the times of his greatest joy and most confident hopes, looks large in himself. His thoughts are very busily employed about his own excellencies, how holy he is, how eminent a saint he is, how much better he is than most of his neighbors, how there are few equal to him; and therefore how it must be that God loves him better than most others; how much God distinguishes him, how much he experiences, and how good he is, and what delight he takes in them on that account.

But the *true spiritual comfort* works in another way. Gracious joy and poverty of spirit go hand in hand, and rejoice, as it were, in each other's company. The godly may at some times have comforts and joys which do not accompany such abasement. They may be lifted up with joy and conceit of, and confidence in, themselves at the same time. But those joys are not spiritual; they are hypocritical joys. Such comforts are not from the Spirit of God. A godly man may have false joys. He is liable to this exercise of corruption, as well as others. And there may be a mixture of one with the other, or false joy and pride may take occasion from true ones, afterwards to appear. But a gracious joy is linked together with poverty of spirit, and never forsakes it.

2. And hence, you may try this by examining what your hopes and comforts are built upon; whether on Christ only, or on your own righteousness. If you would know of what kind your comforts are, follow them up to the fountain, and see what is their source and spring. If you would know of what kind your hope is, examine the bottom of it, and see upon what foundation it stands. If your hope is that which has been given you in the valley of Achor, your own righteousness is not the foundation of it. Inquire therefore what it is which gives you ease with respect to your past sins, what it is which quiets your conscience about them. Is it any sense you have of the free and sovereign and infinite grace and mercy of God in Christ? Is it what you have seen in Christ, or the gospel of his grace, which has lightened your burden with respect to your sins? Or is it that now you think yourself that you have done such and such things, or have met with such things, have such workings of affection toward God, that you are become lovely in his sight, so that he, seeing what holy affections and experiences your heart has been filled with, and what discoveries you have had, he is on that account reconciled to you, and you are become lovely in his eyes? What makes you hope

that you are in favor with God? Is it because you conceive of God as looking down from heaven upon your heart, on your gracious experiences, and so being, as it were, taken with, and receiving you into his favor on account of that? Or is your hope of God's favor built on a sense which you have of Christ's worthiness, and the saving mercy of God in him, and his faithfulness to the promises which he has made through him?

3. Inquire concerning the effect of your comforts, whether they cause an ardent disposition and desire to exalt God and to lie low before him. *True comforts and joys*, which are from the Spirit of God and are well founded, are wont to work after this manner. They excite an inward, intense desire that God may be exalted, and to lie in the dust; such a one as the psalmist seems to have had when he says: "Not unto us, not unto us, but unto thy name give glory" (Ps. 115:1). The repeating of the expression seems to show how ardent his heart was. When God is pleased to lift up the light of his countenance upon the soul, and to impart inward sweetness from a manifestation of his glory, there is wont to be an inward longing to be in the dust. At such times the Christian sees how it becomes him to be humble, and how worthy God and Christ are of all the glory, more than he does at other times. He perceives and laments that he cannot bow enough; that he is not abased as low before God as becomes such a sinner as himself. Hence arises an intense desire after self-abasement; and the soul breathes and pants after humiliation before God.

Examine if hope and comfort have come from the slaying of sin

Inquire whether your hope and comfort are such as have arisen on the slaying of sin. If your hope is that which you obtained before this, you obtained it too soon, and had better be without it than with it. It is not sufficient evidence of your hope that it was given after much trouble and great terrors, or great relentings of heart for sin and bewailing that you had done so wickedly, or that it was after reformations and abstaining from former ways of sin, and a total reformation of some particular evil practices. But if it be a *true hope*, it was given after the slaying of sin. And in order the better to determine this point, let the following inquiries be made.

1. Whether your hope has been accompanied with a heart and a life turned from sin? Or is there no remarkable difference in this respect now from what there was before? We all own conversion to be a great change; and we have all been sufficiently taught that the change consists in this: in turning from sin to God. Therefore there must be a great change in this respect. Is there a great change in this respect in you? I do not inquire whether there be a great change in you in respect to hope and comfort; that whereas formerly you did not suppose yourself to be in Christ and had no hope of it, now you have hope, and a confident hope, which oftentimes is an occasion of new and peculiar joy and elevation of spirit. There may be a great change in you in this respect, and yet you may remain in a Christless

state. But is there a great change with respect to the turning of your heart from sin, and against it?

You may reply to this, "I see still abundance of corruption and wickedness in my heart; and so far is it from being delivered from corruption, that I seem at times to discover more than ever." But whether you see more or less corruption in your heart, is your heart turned against that corruption which you see? Is there a great difference in you in this respect from what there used to be with respect to your being turned against your own sin, and finding within yourself a nature opposite to it, a nature to resist it, to carry it as an uneasy burden? And is your heart turned against yourself for it, in abhorrence of yourself and in indignation against yourself? And is your will turned from sin, that, though you find a great deal of corruption in your heart, yet you do not allow it, you keep a strict watch upon it, and will not let it walk at liberty to appear in your life and conversation? Is there no lust harbored which is prevalent in you, and which is neglected and suffered to range and to walk on every side? Is there no sin wittingly tolerated? Do you aim strictly to keep all God's commandments; and is that your actual care and watch, that you may avoid every evil and every false way; and that you may in all things, so far as in you lies, please and honor God? And do you find that this is the tendency of your hope; that your hope has a sanctifying influence upon you, that it turns you against sin and stirs you up to seek after purity from sin? With respect to most who are present who entertain hope, there has been much opportunity for experience in this matter since you have had your hope, so that one would think by an impartial and strict examination you might be able to answer these inquiries.

2. Those of you who have obtained your hope after special and remarkable departures from God should inquire in what manner hope has been restored. Indeed, hypocrites are not so apt to have their hope abated by such things as those who have a true hope. A hypocrite's hopes and false comforts will subsist, and, it may be, continue as lively as ever, under such great sins and such a course of ill practices as, if a godly man should fall into them, would bring him into exceeding darkness. Some hypocrites will live in very immoral ways, and yet keep up their confidence, seem not to have their hope much shaken, and boast of as much comfort and joy at such times as at any other. But this is not the manner of a true comfort. A true comfort, which flows from the exercise and the breathings of the Spirit of God in the heart, must, of necessity, at such times be exceedingly suppressed; and commonly great trouble and darkness is the effect.

But if it has not been altogether thus with you, but you have found that, at times when you have greatly sinned and gone on in ill practices, your hope has decayed, and in the time of it your conscience told you that the way in which you lived was contrary to known rules, and so was in doubt about your hope, but since that you have grown strong again in your hope, inquire in what manner you have obtained hope again. Unsound professors in such cases are not wont to obtain hope again in the same manner as the truly godly do, in a deep humbling for sin, and in slaying the troubler, as has been described. But it may be only this, that now they do better than they did, and so hope comes again. If they lived in a way of some vile sensuality for a time, and afterwards cease to do so, they look on their reformation as an atonement; and so their hope is renewed without humbling or abasement, without any special convictions of the evil of their ways and special repentance, or renewed sense of their own vileness, or any renewed flying to the mercy of God in Christ for refuge, or any further alienation of their hearts from those evil ways in which they have walked. If your comforts and confidence have been renewed after remarkable aberrations from the way of duty without something of this nature, it is to be feared that you make your own righteousness the ground of your hope and comfort.

3. Inquire whether at those times when you have most hope and comfort above all others, you are not disposed to be careful to avoid sin, and to strive to live holy. Sometimes the hope of hypocrites is very confident; and therefore the degree of confidence which attends a hope is no certain evidence of its truth and genuineness. But we should examine what effect this strong confidence has upon us. Do we find, when our hope is strong and we are most satisfied that our condition is safe, that then we are least careful to avoid sin, and are least disposed to take pains to curb our lusts and resist temptation, or lay ourselves in the way of duty? If it be thus, it is a very bad sign and a black mark on our hopes and comforts. A true hope has a tendency to prompt him who has it to purify himself

and watch and strive more earnestly against all impurity: "He that hath this hope in him purifieth himself" (1 John 3:3). They are condemned who, because they think they are righteous and so that they shall certainly have eternal life, will trust in that hope to give themselves the greater liberty in sin: "When I shall say to the righteous, that he shall surely live; if he trust to his own righteousness, and commit iniquity, all his righteousness shall not be remembered: but for his iniquity that he committed, he shall die" (Ezek. 33:13).

USE OF DIRECTION

If it be so that God is wont to cause hope and comfort to arise after trouble and humbling for sin, and upon slaying of the trouble, this may be of direction to souls under spiritual trouble and darkness, what course to pursue for hope and comfort.

Renounce and forsake sinful behavior

Thoroughly renounce and forsake all ways of sinful behavior. For you have heard that hope and comfort are never to be expected till sin is slain or forsaken. He who is not thorough in his reformation cannot reasonably hope for comfort, how much soever he may abound in some particular duties. Persons who are under awakenings and would seek a true hope of salvation, should in the first place see that they renounce every wicked practice. They should search their ways and consider what is wrong in them: what duties they have omitted which ought to have been done; and what practices they have allowed which ought to be forsaken; and should immediately reform, retaining no way of sin, denying all ungodliness, omitting nothing which is required; and should see that they persevere in it, that it be not merely a temporary, short-lived restraint, but an everlasting renunciation. This is the way to have the troubler slain.

Earnestly to seek humiliation

To that end they should labor to be convinced of sin. They should be much engaged in searching their own hearts and keeping a watchful eye upon them. They should not rest in their own efforts, but earnestly seek to God to give them a right sight of themselves and a right conviction of sin, and show them that they have deserved God's everlasting wrath. And in order to this they should carefully watch against backsliding; for backsliding prevents humiliation. If there has been any progress made by the conviction of God's Spirit toward it, it is all lost by backsliding. This again blinds and stupefies the heart, and sets the man further than ever from a right knowledge of himself and sight of his own heart.

Search out the troubler

Search and endeavor to find out the troubler. You have heard that when the godly are in darkness, it is not for want of love in God to them, or a readiness in him to give them comfort; but that sin is doubtless the cause of their darkness in one way or another. Their troubler lies at their own door. There is doubtless some troubler in the camp, which causes God to withdraw. And therefore, if you would have light revive and have the comfortable presence of God again, the first thing which you do must be to search and to find out the troubler.

Many, when they are in darkness, proceed in a wrong way. They go to examining past experience. And that they should do; but what is wrong in it is that they do that only. They spend their time in seeking for something in themselves which is good; whereas they ought to spend more of it in seeking out that which is bad. Whatever good there is, they are never likely to find it out till they find out the sin which obscures and hides it. And whatever they reflect upon which they formerly thought was good, is not likely to afford any satisfaction to them till that bad thing be removed out of the way which troubled them. They wonder what the cause is that they are so in the dark. They verily thought in time past that they were right, and that they had experienced a right work of God's Spirit on their hearts, and thought that they were the children of God. But now God hides his face from them, and they wonder what is the matter, as Joshua seemed to be so astonished when Israel was smitten down at Ai. Sometimes they almost conclude that it is because they are not the children of God. They pray to God to renew his comforts to them, and spend much time. And they ought to pray. But they have more need to do something else. Joshua spent a great deal of time in prayer when Israel was troubled. He fell upon his face till eventide, complaining to God about his withdrawing from them. But God says to him: "Get thee up; wherefore liest thou upon thy face?" (Josh. 7:10). As much as to say, you had more need to be doing something else than lie there. "Israel hath sinned, and they have also transgressed my covenant which I commanded them; for they have even taken of the accursed thing" (Josh. 7:11). And verse 13: "Up, sanctify yourselves."

This teaches you, who are under darkness and have your hopes darkened and comforts deadened, what you should do. You must arise and search and find out the troubler. If you do not do this, it will signify nothing to you to lie crying and complaining to God about your darkness. You have other business which you have more need to do, though prayer should not be left undone.

Let me beseech you, therefore, to be thorough in this. You have need to be thorough, for it is an exceedingly difficult thing to find out the accursed thing in such cases. Men's hearts do like Achan, who hid the accursed thing in the earth in the midst of his tent (Josh. 7:21). He hid it very closely. He did not content himself with hiding it in the most secret place in his tent, but he dug in the ground and buried it in the earth under his feet, that there might be no sign of it above ground. So are men's deceitful hearts wont to hide the accursed thing which troubles them. When they are put upon searching for the cause of their trouble and darkness, they think of one thing and another, but commonly overlook the chief cause of all their trouble. It does not so much as enter their minds. They search the tent, but that is not enough; they must search the very ground, or they will not find it out. When they tell of their darkness and are put upon searching to see whether some sinful way is not the cause, they readily own that it is their fault. But yet they mistake the true Achan, notwithstanding all they confess of the corruption of their hearts. It is not merely corruption in their hearts, working in their thoughts, which is the cause; but it is some way of outward sin and wickedness, in which they have of late in a great measure allowed themselves. That is the principal cause of their trouble: some way of pride or covetousness, or some way of envy or evil-speaking, or ill will to their neighbors, or self-will, or some other way of unsuitable carriage which is the chief cause of their darkness.

In some respects, it is a great deal easier to find out little sins than greater sins, which causes many to strain at a gnat who swallow a camel. Sins which are common to all and of which all complain, such as corrupt workings of heart, they are willing to feel that it is no disgrace to have them. And the godly commonly tell of such things, and it does not affright them to see them. But such things as malice, a proud behavior, and many other things which might be mentioned, are disagreeable. They are not willing to see such things in themselves. They therefore call them by good names, and put good constructions on them, and hide them, as Achan did his accursed thing, underground. The sin which troubles them most, has greatest possession of their hearts, and does most blind and prejudice their minds is passed over.

They can soon enough discover and see such things in others, in one of the opposite party or the like, but they cannot see them in themselves; and so they continue still under darkness.

It is an exceedingly difficult thing to find out the troubler. You have need, therefore, to be exceedingly thorough in searching for this matter, and not to spare yourself or bribe your conscience at all, but labor to be impartial in the search. And to induce you to this, consider what God said to Joshua: "Neither will I be with you any more, unless you destroy the accursed thing from among you" (Josh. 7:12).

Be thorough to destroy the troubler

And, therefore, when you have found out the troubler, be sure thoroughly to destroy it. Renounce it with detestation, as a vile serpent that has secretly lain under your head for a long time, and infected you with his poisons time after time, and bit you when you were asleep, made you sick and filled you with pain, and you knew it not. Would not a man, when he has found out the serpent in such a case, destroy it with indignation and be forever afterwards thoroughly watchful that he is not caught with such a calamity again? You cannot be too thorough in destroying such an enemy and laboring to root it out and extirpate all its race. Whoever of you are under darkness and trouble, I am bold to say, if God help you to follow these directions, your darkness will soon be scattered, and hope and comfort will arise. And this is the surest and readiest and most direct course which any of you can take in order to the renewing of comfort in your soul. And without this, do not promise yourself any considerable degree of light or comfort while you live, however many examinations of past experiences and prayers to God for light you may make.

STUDY QUESTIONS

1. Let's review all that we have seen thus far in these two sermons. We are called to pursue holiness in the Lord, for this is where the life of blessedness, of increasing joy and comfort and hope, is to be found. The apostle Paul is the prime example of why and how we may take up this, our part, in God's work of sanctification. From the first sermon, how does Paul's example instruct us in the way of holiness? What did you find to be most important for your own journey?

2. The second sermon shows us that our joy and comfort— our happiness in the pursuit of holiness—can be interrupted from time to time by seasons of darkness, spiritual deadness, and wandering from God. Why does this happen to us? Why, according to Edwards (chapter 10) does God allow this to happen?

3. It is a good idea for us always to be examining our hope, joy, and comfort—asking ourselves what is their source or foundation—for there is such a thing as false hope and false comfort. According to Edwards, how would you explain what *false* hope and comfort are?

4. Review the sections in this chapter on self-examination and direction. Then offer a comment or two on the use of each of the following in these important works:

    a. prayer and meditation:
    b. self-watch:
    c. searching the Scriptures:
    d. seeking the counsel of godly friends:

5. Why is Edwards so insistent upon being "thorough" in the destruction of the troubler of our souls? How does he instruct us to do this? The work of sanctification—the journey toward holiness in the Lord—obviously takes a good deal of time—*all* of it, in fact! In what ways is your own time consciously and deliberately devoted to pursuing holiness in the Lord?

❖ *Part 3* ❖

THE PRECIOUSNESS OF TIME AND THE IMPORTANCE OF REDEEMING IT

❈ *Chapter 12* ❈

THE PRECIOUSNESS OF TIME

Sanctification and the pursuit of holiness in the Lord take place in time. Time is a precious gift of God, and we are called to be good stewards of the time he gives us. In this sermon, Edwards shows us why time is so precious, and points us to ways in which we fail in our stewardship of this great gift.

EPHESIANS 5:16
Redeeming the time, because the days are evil.

Christians should not only study to improve the opportunities they enjoy for their *own* advantage, as those who would make a good bargain; but also labor to reclaim *others* from their evil courses; that so God might defer his anger, and time might be redeemed from that terrible destruction which, when it should come, would put an end to the time of divine patience. And it may be upon this account that this reason is added: *Because the days are evil.* As if the apostle had said the corruption of the times tends to hasten threatened judgments; but your holy and circumspect walk will tend to redeem time from the devouring jaws of those calamities. However, this much is certainly held forth to us in the words, *namely*, that upon time we should set a high value and be exceeding careful that it be not lost; and we are therefore exhorted to exercise wisdom and circumspection in order that we may redeem it. And hence it appears, that *time is exceedingly precious*.

Why Time is Precious

Time is precious for the following reasons.

Eternity depends on it

A happy or miserable eternity depends on the good or ill improvement of it. Things are precious in proportion to their importance, or to the degree wherein they concern our welfare. Men are wont to set the highest value on those things upon which they are sensible their interest chiefly depends. And this renders time so exceedingly precious, because our eternal welfare depends on the improvement of it. Indeed, our welfare in *this* world depends upon its improvement. If we improve it not, we shall be in danger of coming to poverty and disgrace; but by a good improvement of it, we may obtain those things which will be useful and comfortable. But it is above all things precious, as our state through eternity depends on it. The importance of the improvement of time upon other accounts is subordinate to this.

Gold and silver are esteemed precious by men; but they are of no worth to any man, only as thereby he has an opportunity of avoiding or removing some evil, or of possessing himself of some good. And the greater the evil is which any man hath advantage to escape, or the good which he hath advantage to obtain, by anything that he possesses, by so much the greater is the value of that thing to him, whatever it be. Thus if a man, by anything which he hath, may save his life, which he most lose without it, he will look upon that by which he hath the opportunity of escaping so great an evil as death to be very precious. Hence it is that time is so exceedingly precious, because by it we have opportunity of escaping everlasting misery and of obtaining everlasting blessedness and glory. On this depends our escape from an infinite evil, and our attainment of an infinite good.

Time is very short

Time is very short, which is another thing that renders it very precious. The scarcity of any commodity occasions men to set a higher value upon it, especially if it be necessary and they cannot do without it. Thus, when Samaria was besieged by the Syrians, and provisions were exceedingly scarce, "an ass's head was sold for fourscore pieces of silver, and the fourth part of a cab of dove's dung for five pieces of silver" (2 Kings 6:25). So time is the more to be prized by men because a whole eternity depends upon it; and yet we have but a little of time. "When a few years are come, then I shall go the way whence I shall not return" (Job 16:22). "My days are swifter than a post. They are passed away as the swift ships; as the eagle that hasteth to the prey" (Job 9:25–26). "Our life; what is it? It is but a vapor which appeareth for a little time, and then vanisheth away" (James 4:14). It is but as a moment to eternity. Time is so short, and the work which we have to do in it is so great, that we have none of it to spare. The work which we have to do to prepare for eternity must be done in time, or it never can be done; and it is found to be a work of great difficulty and labor, and therefore that for which time is the more requisite.

Time is uncertain

Time ought to be esteemed by us very precious, because we are uncertain as to its continuance. We know that it is very short, but we know not how short. We know not how little of it remains, whether a year, or several years, or only a month, a week, or a day. We are every day uncertain whether that day will not be the last, or whether we are to have the whole day. There is nothing that we experience that doth more verify than this: If a man had but little provision laid up for a journey or a voyage, and at the same time knew that if his provision should fail, he must perish by the way, he would be the more choice of it. How much more would many men prize their time if they knew that they had but a few months, or a few days, to live! And certainly a wise man will prize his time the more as he knows not but that it will be so as to himself. This is the case with multitudes now in the world, who at present enjoy health and see no signs of approaching death: many such, no doubt, are to die the next month, many the next week, yea, many probably tomorrow, and some this night; yet these same persons know nothing of it, and perhaps think nothing of it, and neither they nor their neighbors can say that they are more likely soon to be taken out of the world than others. This teaches us how we ought to prize our time, and how careful we ought to be, that we lose none of it.

Time cannot be recovered when past

Time is very precious because, when it is past, it cannot be recovered. There are many things which men possess which, if they part with, they can obtain them again. If a man have parted with something which he had, not knowing the worth of it, or the need he should have of it, he often can regain it, at least with pains and cost. If a man have been overseen in a bargain, and have bartered away or sold something, and afterwards repent of it, he may often obtain a release and recover what he had parted with. But it is not so with respect to time; when once that is gone, it is gone forever; no pains, no cost will recover it. Though we repent ever so much that we let it pass and did not improve it while we had it, it will be to no purpose. Every part of it is successively offered to us that we may choose whether we will make it our own or not. But there is no delay; it will not wait upon us to see whether or not we will comply with the offer. But if we refuse, it is immediately taken away and never offered more. As to that part of time which is gone, however we have neglected to improve it, it is out of our possession and out of our reach.

If we have lived fifty, or sixty, or seventy years and have not improved our time, now it cannot be helped; it is eternally gone from us; all that we can do is to improve the little that remains. Yea, if a man have spent all his life but a few moments unimproved, all that is gone is lost, and only those few remaining moments can possibly be made his own; and if the whole of a man's time be gone, and it be all lost, it is irrecoverable.

Eternity depends on the improvement of time; but when once the time of life is gone, when once death is come, we have no more to do with time; there is no possibility of obtaining the restoration of it, or another space in which to prepare for eternity. If a man should lose the whole of his worldly substance and become a bankrupt, it is possible that his loss may be made up. He may have another estate as good. But when the time of life is gone, it is impossible that we should ever obtain another such time. All opportunity of obtaining eternal welfare is utterly and everlastingly gone.

REFLECTIONS ON TIME PAST

You have now heard of the preciousness of time; and you are the persons concerned, to whom God has committed that precious talent. You have an eternity before you. When God created you and gave you reasonable souls, he made you for an endless duration. He gave you time here in order to a preparation for eternity, and your future eternity depends on the improvement of time. Consider, therefore, what you have done with your *past* time. You are not now beginning your time, but a great deal is past and gone; and all the wit and power and treasure of the universe cannot recover it. Many of you may well conclude that more than half of your time is gone; though you should live to the ordinary age of man, your glass is more than half run, and it may be there are but few sands remaining. Your sun is past the meridian, and perhaps just setting, or going into an everlasting eclipse. Consider, therefore, what account you can give of your improvement of past time. How have you let the precious golden sands of your glass run?

Every day, every moment precious

Every *day* that you have enjoyed has been precious; yea, your *moments* have been precious. But have you not wasted your precious moments, your precious days, yea, your precious years? If you should reckon up how many days you have lived, what a sum would there be! And how precious has every one of those days been! Consider, therefore, what have you done with them? What is become of them all? What can you show of any improvement made, or good done, or benefit obtained, answerable to all this time which you have lived? When you look back and search, do you not find this past time of your lives in a great measure empty, having not been filled up with any good improvement? And if God, who has given you your time, should now call you to an account, what account could you give to him?

Time improved?

How much may be done in a year! How much good is there opportunity to do in such a space of time! How much service may persons do for God, and how much for their own souls, if to their utmost they improve it! How much may be done in a day! But what have you done in so many days and years that you have lived? What have you done with the whole time of your youth, you that are past your youth? Has it not all been in vain to you? Would it not have been as well or better for you if all that time you had been asleep, or in a state of non-existence?

You have had much time of leisure and freedom from worldly business; consider to what purpose you have spent it. You have not only had ordinary time, but you have had a great deal of holy time. What have you done with all the Sabbath days which you have enjoyed? Consider those things seriously, and let your own consciences make answer.

WHO ARE TO BE REPROVED FOR NOT IMPROVING TIME

How little is the preciousness of time considered, and how little sense of it do the greater part of mankind seem to have! And to how little good purpose do many spend their time! There is nothing more precious, and yet nothing of which men are more prodigal. Time is with many as silver was in the days of Solomon, *as the stones of the street, and nothing accounted of.* They act as if time were as plenty as silver was then, and as if they had a great deal more than they needed and knew not what to do with it. If men were as lavish of their money as they are of their time, if it were as common a thing for them to throw away their money as it is for them to throw away their time, we should think them beside themselves and not in the possession of their right minds. Yet time is a thousand times more precious than money; and when it is gone, it cannot be *purchased for money*, cannot be redeemed by silver or gold.

There are several sorts of persons who are reproved by this doctrine, whom I shall particularly mention.

Those who are idle

There are those who spend a great deal of their time in *idleness*, or doing nothing that turns to any account, either for the good of their souls or bodies; nothing either for their own benefit, or for the benefit of their neighbor, either of the family or of the body politic to which they belong. There are some persons upon whose hands time seems to lie heavy, who, instead of being concerned to improve it as it passes, and taking care that it not pass without making it their own, act as if it were rather their concern to contrive ways how to waste and consume it; as though time, instead of being precious, were rather a mere encumbrance to them. Their hands refuse to labor, and rather than put themselves to it, they will let their families suffer, and will suffer themselves: "An idle soul shall suffer hunger" (Prov. 19:15). And: "Drowsiness shall clothe a man with rags" (Prov. 23:21).

Some spend much of their time at the tavern, over their cups, and in wandering about from house to house, wasting away their hours in idle and unprofitable talk which will turn to no good account: "In all labor there is profit; but the talk of the lips tendeth only to poverty" (Prov. 14:23). The direction of the apostle, in Ephesians 4:28, is that we should "labor, working with our hands the thing that is good, that we may have to give to him that needeth." But indolent men, instead of gaining anything to give to him that needeth, do but waste what they have already: "He that is slothful in his work, is brother to him that is a great waster" (Prov. 18:9).

Those who are wicked

They are reproved by this doctrine who spend their time in *wickedness*, who do not merely spend their time in doing nothing to any good purpose, but spend it to ill purposes. Such do not only lose their time, but they do worse; with it they hurt themselves and others. Time is precious, as we have heard, because eternity depends upon it. By the improvement of time we have eternal blessedness. But those who spend their time in wicked works not only neglect to improve their time to obtain eternal happiness or to escape damnation, but they spend it to a quite contrary purpose, namely, to increase their eternal misery, or to render their damnation the more heavy and intolerable.

Some spend time in reveling, and in unclean talk and practices, in vicious company-keeping, in corrupting and ensnaring the minds of others, setting bad examples, and leading others into sin, undoing not only their own souls, but the souls of others. Some spend much of their precious time in detraction and backbiting; in talking against others; in contention, not only quarreling themselves, but fomenting and stirring up strife and contention. It would have been well for some men, and well for their neighbors, if they had never done anything at all; for then they would have done neither good nor hurt. But now they have done a great deal more hurt than they have done or ever will do good. There are some persons whom it would have been better for the towns where they live, to have been at the charge of maintaining them in doing nothing, if that would have kept them in a state of inactivity.

Those who have spent much of their time in wickedness, if ever they shall reform and enter upon a different mode of living, will find not only that they have wasted the past, but that they have made work for their remaining time, to undo what they have done. How will many men, when they shall have done with time and shall look back upon their past lives, wish that they had had no time! The time which they spend on earth will be worse to them than if they had spent so much time in hell; for an eternity of dreadful misery in hell will be the fruit of their time on earth, as they employ it.

Those who indulge only in worldly pursuits

Those are reproved by this doctrine who spend their time only in *worldly* pursuits, neglecting their souls. Such men lose their time, let them be ever so diligent in their worldly business, and though they may be careful not to let any of it pass so, but that it shall some way or other turn to their worldly profit. They that improve time only for their benefit in time, lose it; because time was not given for itself, but for that everlasting duration which succeeds it.

They, therefore, whose time is taken up in caring and laboring for the world only, in inquiring what they shall eat, and what they shall drink, and wherewithal they shall be clothed; in contriving to lay up for themselves treasures upon earth, how to enrich themselves, how to make themselves great in the world, or how to live in comfortable and pleasant circumstances while here; who busy their minds and employ their strength in these things only, and the stream of whose affections is directed toward these things; lose their precious time.

Let such, therefore, as have been guilty of thus spending their time consider it. You have spent a great part of your time, and a great part of your strength, in getting a little of the world; and how little good doth it afford you, now you have gotten it! What happiness or satisfaction can you reap from it? Will it give you peace of conscience, or any rational quietness or comfort? What is your poor, needy, perishing soul the better for it? And what better prospects doth it afford you of your approaching eternity? And what will all that you have acquired avail you when time shall be no longer?

STUDY QUESTIONS

1. In this sermon Edwards makes the point that we will either invest our time for eternity or squander it in the

affairs of the merely present. Time, he says, is a precious gift. What makes time so precious? Have you ever considered this before?

2. Imagine that you had an unlimited account of time that you could recover—time from your past days, weeks, months, years. Spend a few moments reflecting on the second section of this chapter—on time past. Think back over just the past year of your life. How much of that unlimited account of time would you spend in order to recover some of this past year? Why?

3. "If men were as lavish of their money as they are of their time, if it were as common a thing for them to throw away their money as it is for them to throw away their time, we should think them beside themselves and not in possession of their right minds." What are some ways in which we "throw away" our time? Do you find any of these in your life?

4. Edwards warns three groups of people that they are in danger of this "doctrine" (teaching) about the preciousness of time: the idle, the wicked, and the merely worldly. Do you see any aspects of any of these people in your own life? Explain.

5. Edwards mentioned "ordinary" and "holy" time. What do you suppose he means by these terms? How much of your time each day is "ordinary"? How much is "holy"? Do you think you have a proper balance of these? Explain.

❈ *Chapter 13* ❈

IMPROVING TIME

Edwards calls us to use our time as wise stewards, making the most of the time we have been given, redeeming it for good works of love to God and our neighbors. He is not espousing a doctrine of salvation by works, but salvation demonstrated in works. In this final section, Edwards now shows us how to improve the time God has given us for the pursuit of holiness in the Lord.

AN EXHORTATION TO IMPROVE TIME

Consider what has been said of the preciousness of time, how much depends upon it, how short and uncertain it is, how irrecoverable it will be when gone. If you have a right conception of these things, you will be more choice of your time than of the most fine gold. Every hour and moment will seem precious to you. But besides these considerations which have been already set before you, consider also the following.

We are accountable to God for our time

You are accountable to God for your time. Time is a talent given us by God; he has set us our day, and it is not for nothing; our day was appointed for some work; therefore he will, at the day's end, call us to an account. We must give account to him of the improvement of all our time.

We are God's servants; as a servant is accountable to his master how he spends his time when he is sent forth to work, so are we accountable to God. If men would aright consider this and keep it in mind, would they not improve their time otherwise than they do? Would you not behave otherwise than you do, if you considered with yourselves every morning that you must give an account to God how you shall have spent that day? And if you considered with yourselves at the beginning of every evening that you must give an account to God how you shall have spent that evening? Christ has told us that "for every idle word which men speak, they shall give an account in the day of judgment" (Matt. 12:36). How well, therefore, may we conclude that we must give an account of all our idle, misspent time!

How much time we have lost already

Consider how much time you have lost already. For your having lost so much, you have the greater need of diligently improving what yet remains. You ought to mourn and lament over your lost time; but that is not all, you must apply yourselves the more diligently to improve the remaining part, that you may redeem lost time. You who are considerably advanced in life, and have hitherto spent your time in vanities and worldly cares, and have lived in a great measure negligent of the interests of your souls, may well be terrified and amazed when you think how much time you have lost and wasted away. In that you have lost so much time, you have the more need of diligence, on three accounts.

1. As your opportunity is so much the shorter. Your time at its whole length is short. But set aside all that you have already lost, and then how much shorter is it! As to that part of your time which you have already lost, it is not to be reckoned into your opportunity, for that will never be any more; and it is no better, but worse to you than if it never had been.

2. You have the same work to do that you had at first, and that under greater difficulties. Hitherto you have done nothing at all of your work; all remains to be done, and that with vastly greater difficulties and opposition in your way than would have been if you had set about it seasonably. So that the time in which to do your work is not only grown shorter, but your work is grown greater. You not only have the *same* work to do, but you have *more* work; for while you have lost your time, you have not only shortened it, but you have been making work for yourselves. How well may this consideration awaken you to a thorough care not to let things run on in this manner any longer, and rouse

you up immediately to apply yourselves to your work with all your might!

3. That is the best of your time which you have lost. The first of a man's time, after he comes to the exercise of his reason and to be capable of performing his work, is the best. You who have lived in sin till past your youth have lost the best part. So that here are all these things to be considered together, namely, that your time in the whole is but short, there is none to spare; a great part of that is gone, so that it is become much shorter; that which is gone is the best; yet all your work remains, and not only so, but with greater difficulties than ever before attended it; and the shorter your time is, the more work you have to do.

What will make you sensible of the necessity of a diligent improvement of remaining time, if these things will not? Sometimes such considerations as these have another effect, namely, to discourage persons, and to make them think that, seeing they have lost so much time, it is not worth their while to attempt to do anything now. The devil makes fools of them; for when they are young, he tells them there is time enough hereafter, there is no need of being in haste, it will be better seeking salvation hereafter; and then they believe him. Afterwards, when their youth is past, he tells them that it is not worth their while to attempt to do anything; and now they believe him too. So that with them no time is good. The season of youth is not a good time; for that is most fit for pleasure and mirth, and there will be time enough afterwards; and what comes afterwards is not a good time, because the best of it is gone. Thus are men infatuated and ruined.

But what madness is it for persons to give way to discouragement, so as to neglect their work, because their time is short! What need have they rather to awake out of sleep, thoroughly to rouse up themselves, and to be in good earnest that, if possible, they may yet obtain eternal life! Peradventure God may yet give them repentance to the acknowledgment of the truth, that they may be saved. Though it be late in the day, yet God calls upon you to rouse and to apply yourself to your work; and will you not hearken to *his* counsel in this great affair, rather than to the counsel of your mortal enemy?

The preciousness of time to those near its end

Consider how time is sometimes valued by those who are come near to the end of it. What a sense of its preciousness have poor sinners sometimes when they are on their death beds! Such have cried out, *O, a thousand worlds for an inch of time!* Then time appears to them indeed precious. An inch of time could do them no more good than before, when they were in health, supposing a like disposition to improve it, nor indeed so much; for a man's time upon a death bed is attended with far greater disadvantage for such an improvement as will be for the good of his soul, than when he is in health. But the near approach of death makes men sensible of the inestimable worth of time. Perhaps, when they were in health, they were as insensible of its value as you are, and were as negligent of it. But how are their thoughts altered now! It is not because they are deceived that they think time to be of such value, but because their eyes are opened; and it is because you are deceived and blind that you do not think as they do.

The preciousness of time to those past time

Consider what a value we may conclude is set upon time by those who are past the end of it. What thoughts do you think they have of its preciousness, who have lost all their opportunity for obtaining eternal life and are gone to hell? Though they were very lavish of their time while they lived, and set no great value upon it, yet how have they changed their judgments! How would they value the opportunity which *you* have, if they might but have it granted to *them*! What would they not give for one of your days under the means of grace! So will you, first or last, be convinced. But if you be not convinced except in the manner in which they are, it will be too late.

There are two ways of making men sensible of the preciousness of time. One is by showing them the reason why it must be precious, by telling them how much depends on it, how short it is, how uncertain, and so forth. The other is experience, wherein men are convinced how much depends on the improvement of time. The latter is the most effectual way; for that always convinces, if nothing else doth. But if persons be not convinced by the former means, the latter will do them no good. If the former be ineffectual, the latter, though it be certain, yet is always too late. Experience never fails to open the eyes of men, though they were never opened before. But if they be first opened by that, it is no way to their benefit. Let all therefore be persuaded to improve their time to their utmost.

ADVICE FOR IMPROVING TIME

I shall conclude with advising to three things in particular.

Improve the present without delay

Improve the *present* time without any delay. If you delay and put off its improvement, still more time will be lost, and it will be an evidence that you are not sensible of its preciousness. Talk not of more convenient seasons hereafter, but improve your time while you have it, after the example of the psalmist: "I made haste, and delayed not to keep thy commandments" (Ps. 119:60).

Improve the most precious parts of time

Be especially careful to improve *those parts* of time which are most precious. Though all time is precious, yet some parts are more precious than others; as, particularly, holy time is more precious than common time. Such time is of great advantage for your everlasting welfare; therefore, above all, improve your Sabbaths, and especially the time of public worship, which is the most precious part. Lose it not either in sleep or in carelessness, inattention, and wandering imaginations. How sottish are they who waste away not only their common, but holy time, yea the very season of attendance on the holy ordinances of God! The time of youth is precious on many accounts. Therefore, if you be in the enjoyment of this time, take heed that you improve it. Let not the precious days and years of youth slip away without improvement. A time of the strivings of God's Spirit is more precious than other time. Then God is near; and we are directed, in Isaiah 55:6, to "seek the Lord while he may be found, and to call upon him while he is near." Such especially is an accepted time and a day of salvation: "I have heard of thee in a time accepted, and in a day of salvation I have succored thee: behold, now is the accepted time; behold, now is the day of salvation" (2 Cor. 6:2).

Improve leisure time

Improve well your time of *leisure* from worldly business. Many persons have a great deal of such time, and all have some. If men be but disposed to it, such time may be improved to great advantage. When we are most free from cares of the body and business of an outward nature, a happy opportunity for the soul is afforded. Therefore spend not such opportunities unprofitably, nor in such a manner that you will not be able to give a good account thereof to God. Waste them not away wholly in unprofitable visits, or useless diversions or amusements. Diversion should be used only in subserviency to business. So much, and no more, should be used as doth most fit the mind and body for the work of our general and particular callings.

You have need to improve every talent, advantage, and opportunity to your utmost, while time lasts; for it will soon be said concerning you, according to the oath of the angel in Revelation 10:5–6, "And the angel which I saw stand upon the sea and upon the earth lifted up his hand to heaven, and sware by him that liveth forever and ever, who created heaven, and the things that therein are, and the earth, and the things that therein are, and the sea, and the things which therein are, *that there should be time no longer.*"

STUDY QUESTIONS

1. Edwards is not calling us to work *in order* to salvation, but *as a consequence and proof* of it. We are not saved by works; however, we are not saved without them. How do the following verses support this idea?

   a. Ephesians 2:8–10:
   b. Philippians 2:12–13:
   c. John 15:16–17:
   d. 2 Peter 1:3–11:

2. The apostle James tells us that the only way we can *prove* that we have saving faith is by the works that we do. How can you see this in his argument in James 2:14–26?

3. Any good works that we might do—good works for which we were created anew in Christ Jesus (Eph. 2:10)—must

be accomplished *in time*. What does Edwards mean by "improving" time? Why should we do so?

4. What would you think of someone who did not think it was necessary to improve time—to *redeem* it and make *better use* of it—for the works and fruit for which the Lord called and saved us? What would you say to persuade such a person? How would you counsel that person to begin *improving* time?

5. Review the goals you set for yourself at the end of chapter 1. Were you able to achieve them? Have you thought of any other goals you might like to set as a result of this study on pursuing holiness in the Lord?

INDEX OF SCRIPTURE

Genesis
12:3—92

Exodus
14:13—116
14:14—117

Deuteronomy
8:2—109
32:15—109

Joshua
7—154
7:10—166
7:11—166
7:12—147, 168
7:13—166
7:21—166
7:24–26—113
7:26—104

2 Kings
6:25—175

Job
9:25–26—175–76

16:22—175
31—34
33:16–30—132
42:6—135

Psalms
30:5—129
38—131
38:2–4—131
42:7—122
51:8—131
51:12—126
51:16–17—135
88:6–7—122
97:11—128–29
104:15—102
115:1—158
119:59—134
119:60—193
137:6—65

Proverbs
14:23—182
18:9—182
19:15—181

23:21—181
31:6—101

Isaiah
24:17–18—106
32:15—103
54:7–8—129
55:6—194
59:1–2—123
61:7—129
66:2—34

Ezekiel
33:13—163

Hosea
2:2—101
2:5—100, 146
2:5–13—100
2:6—143
2:7—143
2:8—146
2:9—146
2:11–12—146
2:12—102, 146

2:14—101
2:14-15—100
2:15—99, 101
2:16—101
2:19-20—101

Matthew
5:48—15
7:13-14—34-35
7:23-33
11:12—28
12:36—188

Acts
9—28
17:6—68
20:7—67
20:11—67
20:22-24—77
20:33—46

Romans
1:8—47-48
1:11-12—58
1:15-16—45
4:12—18
5:5—42
8:35-37—42-43
8:36—76
9:1-3—55
10:1—55
11:33—153
16:19—71

1 Corinthians
3:8—36, 93
4:10—45
4:12-13—54
4:13—45
4:16—18
8:13—72
9:1-6—72
9:16—33
9:25—36
9:26—24
9:27—24, 31, 46
10:33—56
11:1—18
15:10—66
15:31—76

2 Corinthians
1:3-5—89-90
1:8—76
1:12—89
2:4—62
2:14—90
3:6—85
3:12-13—84
4:9-11—75
4:11—40
4:18—46
5:4—46
5:6-8—40
5:14—42
6:2—194
6:4-10—74-75
6:10-11—90

1 Corinthians
7:4—90
7:5—76
7:6-7—57-58
7:8—57
7:11—135, 136
7:13—58
9:6—36
10:12—88
11:2-3—62
11:23-27—75
11:28—67
11:29—57
12—49
12:6—49-50
12:10—46, 94
12:15—54-55
12:16—70

Galatians
6:14—45

Ephesians
1:15-16—48
2:20—84
4:28—182
5:1—15
5:16—173

Philippians
1:3-5—64
1:8—58
1:15-18—63-64
1:20—27
1:21—27

2:1–2—56
2:12—34
2:16–17—63
3—25
3:4–12—35–36
3:8—42, 74
3:8–9—22
3:11–14—26
3:17—13
4:1—58
4:11–13—49

Colossians
1:3—48
1:3–4—64
1:24—77
2:5—63

1 Thessalonians
1:2–3—48
1:3—63
1:6—18

2:6—46
2:9—67
2:20—63
3:6–7—64
3:9–10—48

2 Thessalonians
3:7—18–19

1 Timothy
4:12—82

2 Timothy—76
1:3—48
1:12—40
2:10—76
4:6–7—68
4:6–8—92–93
4:7–8—36

Titus
2:7—82

Hebrews
6:12—17
11—17
11:1—95
13:7—18, 83

James
4:14—176
5:10—18, 84

1 Peter
5:1–3—82

1 John
3:3—163

Revelation
4:9–10—38
10:5–6—195